THE RICHMOND
LOCOMOTIVE & MACHINE WORKS

THE RICHMOND LOCOMOTIVE & MACHINE WORKS

ENGINE OF THE OLD DOMINION

NATHAN VERNON MADISON

THE History PRESS

Published by The History Press
Charleston, SC
www.historypress.com

First published 2023

Manufactured in the United States

ISBN 9781467151795

Library of Congress Control Number: 2022949537

Notice: The information in this book is true and complete to the best of our knowledge. It is offered without guarantee on the part of the author or The History Press. The author and The History Press disclaim all liability in connection with the use of this book.

I have been branded with folly and madness for attempting what the world calls impossibilities. . . . This so far has been my reward from the public. . . . However much I may be straitened in pecuniary circumstances, the great honour of being a useful subject can never be taken from me, which to me far exceeds riches.

—Richard Trevithick, 1833

CONTENTS

ACKNOWLEDGEMENTS

I owe a great deal of thanks to a number of individuals who have aided my efforts over the course of this work, at times made all the more difficult as a result of the late pandemic. I would like to thank the staffs of the Virginia Museum of History & Culture and the Library of Virginia for aid in navigating their vast collections. Kelly Kerney of the Valentine Museum offered invaluable assistance regarding both textual and photographic resources. Kay Peterson and Christine Windheuser of the Smithsonian Institution's National Museum of American History were instrumental in my gaining access to the John H. White Jr. Railroad History Collection, allowing me to present information in this work hitherto unpublished; I am further indebted to them for their assistance in acquiring photographic evidence to further elucidate the history of the Richmond Locomotive Works. My sincerest thanks go to Shane Kasper of Shamrock Environmental, for information he provided, as well as his time guiding me through the remnants of the Locomotive Works' Shockoe Valley site. I am indebted to Jeff Brooks for the information he imparted regarding the history of his family's company, Brooks Transfer and Storage.

I am particularly grateful to my editor at The History Press, Kate Jenkins, who helped immensely along the way, despite my frequent needs for just a tad more time due to COVID restrictions; new information constantly presenting itself; or any other unforeseen circumstances that happened to manifest.

I would like to thank my family—my father, James; my sisters Natalie Madison and Stacey Dunbar; and my brother-in-law, Kevin Dunbar—all of whom, in their own way, have given me encouragement. And thanks to my mother, Sylvia Madison, who throughout the course of her life always supported me in all of my myriad endeavors. Thank you.

INTRODUCTION

Throughout any number of surveys regarding Richmond's industrial heritage, there are several establishments and names that appear frequently, almost as prerequisites. Richmond's long history of tobacco and cigarettes manufacture cannot be broached without mentioning names such as Ginter and Mayo. Flour-milling, among Richmond's earliest industries, is synonymous with the names Gallego, Haxall and Dunlop. The heyday of the River City's prominence in the iron and mechanical engineering trades is largely dominated by three concerns in particular: the Tredegar Iron Works, Old Dominion Iron and Nail Works and the Richmond Locomotive Works. Of the first, much has been written; of the second, very little unfortunately; and of the third, just as little, if not less.

The Richmond Locomotive Works, over the course of six decades and several name, product line, and management changes, grew from a small workshop amid the ruins of the Confederacy's collapse to a modern producer of capital goods, the southernmost outpost of the mammoth American Locomotive Company. It often ranked as Richmond's single largest employer, a payroll totaling 9,000 workmen at its highest, and manufactured over 4,500 locomotives between 1887 and 1927. Yet histories of "the Works," as those who labored in its forges and boiler shops referred to it, can be counted on one hand.

Locomotive historian John H. White Jr., in an article for the Railway and Locomotive Historical Society's journal, *Railroad History* (no. 130, Spring

Advertisement, Richmond Locomotive and Machine Works, 1892. *Nathan Vernon Madison.*

1974) provides an overall, yet relatively brief, history of the company, and it, alongside the locomotive production list he and W.D. Edson compiled, is invaluable to any historian of Richmond's industrial past and serves as the source for much of the Work's order and production history found in these pages. Whereas White's account is largely a straightforward business history, William E. Warden Jr.'s short article in the September 1969 edition of *Railroad Magazine* speaks more to the romanticism of the business and its era, the memories of the workmen who labored inside what, in their minds, was already a legendary institution that helped spur America's economic and industrial growth in the late nineteenth and early twentieth centuries. Warden's interviews, replete with proud reminiscences, are just as significant a historical resource as any statistical list or business ledger. The 2006 application for the Richmond Locomotive Works' entry into the National Register of Historical Places provides vital insight into the locomotive industry of the day and the history of several surviving structures. Unfortunately, it confuses the Works' history with that of a subordinate branch (also in Richmond) to such a degree that, technically, the incorrect building now carries the historical registry, as no locomotives were ever produced in the buildings it references. That being said, I believe there is no better place for the history of the Richmond Locomotive Works to be commemorated publicly. By preserving this extension of the original Shockoe Valley plant, the current stewards of the Accessories Plant (now home to Bow Tie Cinemas' Movieland at Boulevard Square) have done an admirable job of safeguarding the history of the Locomotive Works. Paintings of locomotives produced at the Works adorn the lobby, and throughout artifacts, signage, and industrial remnants convey that history in an environment readily open to the public. Among the city's most popular and well-attended cinemas, it is, in its own unique manner, a fourth record of the Works' history, in and of itself. However, with only these resources, the history of the Locomotive Works has nonetheless remained somewhat muddled and incomplete, a hindrance to any researcher chronicling Richmond's industrial past and one that necessitates a complete, thorough and modern study of the company and its history.

I can freely admit I did not quite appreciate just how spoiled I was when, several years ago, I penned a complete history of the Tredegar Iron Works. It is not an exaggeration in the slightest to say that nearly every receipt, every letter in or out, was retained and preserved for posterity. The wealth of information regarding the Tredegar Company in those records, primarily held at thef Library of Virginia, proved overwhelming and often resulted in the unenviable task of deciding what information I still had the room to convey. No such repository or archives exists for the Richmond Locomotive Works, seemingly due to a 1915 flood that inundated the firm's offices and destroyed many historical and business records. Of surviving documents, a scant few are retained at the Virginia Museum of History & Culture archives, among the personal letterbooks of Joseph Bryan and even fewer at the Library of Virginia; the Valentine Richmond History Museum's assemblage of images of the Works is small, but it is the best in existence. Syracuse University possesses the records of the American Locomotive Company in its collections, but little of that pertains to the Richmond Branch. Alongside the few business and personal records that remain, the Library of Virginia's newspaper collections, as well as those digitized by Virginia Chronicle and the Library of Congress's Chronicling America, have proved vital and are used extensively throughout this work. The Library of Congress's collection of historical Sanborn insurance maps served an instrumental role in understanding the Works' physical dimensions and infrastructure.

Other difficulties in research included individuals or, in some cases, the lack thereof. Lamentably, much of industrial history is dependent on the elites, the captains of industry who steered these behemoths of capital; this is certainly true in the case of the Locomotive Works. Thankfully, albeit to a slightly lesser extent, in the case of the Richmond Locomotive Works, the contributions on the part of select superintendents, engineers, and foremen have also been preserved. The lives and labors of individual workers, however, is not nearly as readily available as a historian would prefer. Union activism, strikes, and workers' benevolent societies, as well as simply the prodigious amount of complex and heavy machinery these men produced daily, must remain the greatest testaments to their labors, for the time being.

In regards to race in Richmond's heavy industries, Tredegar's records contained separate ledgers for White and Black workers; while as disgusting and unfortunate was the belief that such demarcations were necessary, such insight does prove useful to historians regarding the history of southern labor. Such records are, not surprisingly, lacking for the Works, so while it is known African Americans were employed there in significant numbers, what positions they held is unknown for the moment. Census records are of little help in this regard, as many occupational descriptions do not go further in detail beyond "mechanic" or "laborer;" likewise, while employers such as Tredegar appear from time to time in Richmond's historic African American press, such as the *Richmond Planet* and *St. Luke Herald*, only a few mentions of the Richmond Locomotive Works are to be found in the former and none, so far, in the latter. Unfortunately, owing to the racial climate of both the region and the industry at the time, it is unlikely that African Americans, regardless of their skills, held positions such as boilermakers or other titles highly specialized to locomotive production. The long history of first enslaved and then free Black workers throughout Richmond's ironmaking establishments, particularly at Tredegar, makes it quite likely that African Americans at the Richmond Locomotive Works labored as highly skilled foundrymen and other related positions, the talents from which could be transferred to a variety of duties.

Regarding an individual for whom a vast amount of information is readily obtainable, Joseph Bryan's role in the history of the Locomotive Works cannot be disregarded; equally, his understanding of society as viewed through the lens of the Lost Cause and the role he envisioned for the former landed aristocracy of the "New South" should not be overlooked, as it informed much of his business and societal dealings. His views on topics related to race are painful for any historian, or human being in general, to read today. The self-appointed paternalism he viewed as his rightful role in society—which did in some instances benefit many of the workers in his employ—is irrevocably tied to his antebellum upbringing and his adherence to the principles of that upbringing. He should not be glorified for these traits, nor can his role in Richmond's industrial history be ignored.

This is a work of industrial and business history but also of Richmond history. As one of the premier industrial concerns in the city for over half a century, the Locomotive Works played a prominent role in Richmond's economic recovery and growth following the Civil War. The story of the Works, from founding to dissolution, is the story of a particular business, certainly, but also serves as microcosm of American business history overall. A transition from a small workshop to a growing concern managed and funded by local elites, and eventually to its assimilation into a nationwide conglomerate, is a history mirrored countless times across the United States throughout the late nineteenth and early twentieth centuries, the era that witnessed the "corporatizing" and "rationalizing" of American business. For many businesses across the South, Richmond no exception, the southern aristocracy that had largely controlled local industry prior were overtaken by a new managerial class, by corporate leaders stationed thousands of miles away for whom regional pride and societal standing in their subsidiaries' towns meant very little.

Taking the scant business records still extant, combined with historical trade journals, letterbooks, government records, newspaper articles, and individual remembrances, I have endeavored to amalgamate all of these various sources into a single whole, as complete a history as is possible, thus far, of the Richmond Locomotive Works—a history often referenced, but rarely investigated. It is my sincerest hope that my effort does some level of justice to that history.

1

RAILS COME TO RICHMOND AND EARLY ENGINE MANUFACTURERS

1810–1865

The earliest means of travel throughout central Virginia were simple roads created during the colonial era, which while certainly sufficient for travel between small settlements were not conducive to generating wider economic and communication networks; along such roads, it could take up to ten days to travel from Richmond to Baltimore, along a path laden with woodlands, stumps, and other hindrances.[1]

In 1816, the Virginia General Assembly established the Board of Public Works, which was tasked with improving transportation across the Commonwealth, primarily by investing heavily in companies, via private-public partnerships, that sought to construct much-needed infrastructure.[2] Decades prior, in 1785, the James River Company was chartered, with the intention of connecting the James with the Ohio River via the Kanawha River (a tributary of the Ohio located in present-day West Virginia). This would have, if successful, cemented the 350-mile-long James River, which runs through central Virginia to the Chesapeake Bay, as a major shipping lane and establish Virginia as the fledgling republic's economic and commercial center.[3] The project suffered from poor management and financial issues, faltering along for several years and reaching only seven miles west of Richmond, to Westham, before being taken over completely by the Board of Public Works in 1823. The canal fared no better under government supervision, and work was temporarily suspended, until 1832, when the entire effort was reorganized as the James River and Kanawha Canal Company. President of the Canal Company James C. Cabell and its chief engineer, Charles Ellet, oversaw a rapid improvement in the canal's fortunes once work recommenced, with thousands of workmen extending the canal's reach to approximately 197 miles until 1851, when the western terminus at Buchanan in Botetourt County was completed.[4] Although failing in its initial goal to reach the Ohio River, the canal nonetheless aided the development of Richmond into the South's industrial and financial hub, and came to be overshadowed in import only with the growth of railroads.

The earliest known railway in Virginia dates to about 1810, to a site several miles south of Richmond along Falling Creek, a tributary of the James in present-day Chesterfield County.[5] Falling Creek is memorialized today as the home of the first iron works in North America, prior to its destruction during a Native American raid in 1622. However, by the early 1770s, at Falling Creek's junction with Pocoshock Creek and a few miles west of the former iron works, Bavarian immigrant Jacob Rubsamen operated a powder mill. Rubsamen produced gunpowder in support of the Continental army during the Revolutionary War, one of only a handful of such mills in the United States manufacturing this vital resource.[6] Rubsamen's partner in the venture was Archibald Cary, a wealthy landowner and politician who represented Chesterfield County at the first Virginia Convention in August 1774 and used his personal wealth to help underwrite the Virginia militia; it is for Archibald Cary that modern Richmond's famed Cary Street is named. The powder mill was razed not once, but twice by British forces, including during Benedict Arnold's January 1781 raid on Richmond.[7]

Following the end of the war, the powder mill at Falling Creek was rebuilt shortly before the commencement of the War of 1812 under the proprietorship of Brown, Page, & Burr. By 1813, the partners had assured Governor James Barbour that their powder mill, though still under construction, was nonetheless capable of producing 100 pounds per day, with more possible as internal improvements to the plant continued. The work was deemed so necessary that the proprietors requested their workmen be exempt from military duty, to ensure the continued production of gunpowder.[8] The grounds of the mill had within its confines what is considered by many the first railroad in Virginia, a one-mile wooden track, about the width of a handcart, linking the powder magazine to the mill itself, designed by the mill's resident engineer, George Magers.[9] Magers's gravity rail, with an 8 percent gradient and at one point traversing a 75-foot-high trestle, was quite inventive, as it made use of a system wherein one rail was single-flanged and the parallel rail double-flanged, with the cart's wheels constructed so as to compliment their respective sides, allowing for increased stability on the rugged terrain, far more than would have been possible on simpler, non-flanged tracks.[10] To improve navigation, the one cart used on the road, approximately 18 to 20 feet in length, boasted a manual breaking system and was returned uphill, not by beasts of burden but rather a waterwheel-powered drum, which when rotated coiled about itself a rope attached to the cart's rear.[11] Following an explosion at the mill in 1819, local remembrances speak of the Falling Creek Railway surviving for decades thereafter, used by both passengers and, later, as a kind of early rollercoaster for local thrill seekers.[12]

The first railway connecting two differing geographical points in Virginia was constructed for the purposes of facilitating the Richmond area's lucrative bituminous coal industry. The Richmond Coal Basin is a roughly 96,000-acre expanse just west of the James River's fall line in Richmond, spanning Amelia, Chesterfield, Goochland, Hanover, Henrico and Powhatan Counties, with Chesterfield, and the village of Midlothian in particular, square in the center, where the coal is greatest in "thickness and purity."[13] The basin was first mined for coal in the eighteenth century; within several decades, a number of mines were scattered along the basin and were responsible for much of the coal shipped across the country, with one Midlothian mine, Clover Hill, producing an average of 87,500 tons a year between 1822 and 1841.[14] In 1828, the Chesterfield Coalfield Railroad was chartered; the resultant 13-mile gravity rail, designed by Moncure Robinson, improved conveyance to shipping depots in Richmond and Manchester, Richmond's sister city across the James. The tracks were made of wood, and the return trip to the mines was facilitated by mules.[15] The road was a success upon its opening in 1831 and was used to shuttle coal and passengers alike; in December 1833, the line was placing ads in local papers requesting no fewer than 75 "young, active and able-bodied Labourers" at "liberal prices" for work running and maintaining the railroad.[16] The coal basin proved lucrative until the growth of the anthracite coal industry in Pennsylvania in the 1840s.

Even as railroads such as the Chesterfield and others were chartered and began to prove their worth, there was still outcry against them and insinuations that railroads were inferior to canals in every conceivable way, be it in the timely transport of livestock, the safe conveyance of industrial equipment, or the threat of emerging railroad monopolies.[17] While the issue of monopolies within the railroading industry was certainly a valid concern—and one that would appear time and time again over the course of the succeeding century—the reduction in transportation outlays were apparent nearly as soon as a railroad went into operation. Farmers oftentimes argued heavily in favor of railroads, as one of the primary drivers for the growth of commercial railroads in Virginia was not only industry but also agriculture. Fields tilled since the arrival of the first Englishmen in Virginia were facing soil fatigue, unable to produce the abundance of crops once possible, and farms began to spread west as the coastal cities and the Tidewater region's role in the state's agricultural output lessened; farmers demanded faster methods by which to bring livestock and produce to market, the traditional drives and wagon trails not sufficing, and many Virginians cited examples such as New York and Baltimore as to the economic clout railroads could bring to any potential entrepôt.[18]

The Chesterfield Railroad paved the way for several others, such as the Clover Hill Railroad, chartered in 1841 and also for the purposes of ferrying Midlothian coal to docks along the James River.[19] Five major lines soon appeared that traversed Richmond and provided the city with the connections required of a prospective financial and manufacturing center. In 1834, the Richmond, Fredericksburg & Potomac Railroad (RF&P) was granted a charter, and two years later, the line opened for business, with its final connection, through Fredericksburg to Aquia Creek along the Potomac River, completed in September 1842. In 1836, the Richmond & Petersburg Railroad (R&P) was founded, Moncure Robinson once again providing surveying services; two years later, a bridge spanning 2,850 feet across the James River was completed, and the railway was in full operation.[20] Chartered also in 1836 was the Louisa Railroad Company, with the initial goal of connecting the RF&P depot in Taylorsville to Fredericks Hall; within two decades, the Louisa Railroad, rechristened the Virginia Central in 1850, had expanded beyond its original intent and linked Richmond and the Tidewater to the farmlands and ore deposits of the Shenandoah Valley.[21] The Richmond & York River Railroad was founded in 1851, and by 1861 the line had been completed, running engines to and from the town of West Point in King William County, along the York River, around thirty-nine miles east of Richmond.[22] In March 1847, the Richmond & Danville Railroad was chartered, but it was not until May 1856 that a direct line between its eponymous endpoints was completed.[23] This rapid proliferation of railroads in and around Richmond unsurprisingly necessitated the establishment of regional locomotive manufactories.

Engine Manufacturing Begins in Richmond

Founded in 1737 and incorporated in 1742, Richmond's location in central Virginia contains several features that particularly engendered it to the growth of industry. The city is located at the falls of the James River, which allows for connections to coastal markets through the Chesapeake Bay; the construction of the James River and Kanawha Canal augmented the ease of trade between Richmond and the western portions of the state as far as the Appalachians, as well as provided additional points from which waterpower, via raceways and millraces, could be harnessed. As has been noted, numerous coal mines dotted the surrounding counties; canal and later railroad lines facilitated the shipping of coal across the country. Richmond was a hub for the tobacco trade, which understandably led to the establishment of manufactories for loose-leaf and plug tobacco and later cigarettes near the river's edge. Likewise, flour-milling was a chief industry, with thousands of barrels from Richmond mills shipped throughout North and South America each year. As industry matured, machine shops were required to manufacture much-needed tools and equipment, particularly stationary and portable steam engines.

The earliest known locomotive works in Richmond was within the Richmond Foundry, an iron works founded about 1820 by several partners, including David J. Burr, a local businessman who, in years prior, had operated a general store adjacent to Richmond's famed Eagle Tavern between 12th and 13th on Main Street, which sold everything from shoes and hats to imported wines and items produced by inmates at the nearby state penitentiary.[24] Burr was also coincidently the administrator of the estate of the late George Magers, designer of the Falling Creek Railway.[25] Following the dissolution of the partnership within which he had established the Richmond Foundry, located at the intersection of B (modern-day Byrd) and 5th Streets, Burr took sole ownership of the works, manufacturing small iron and brass items, as well as stationary steam engines and presses, before moving on to locomotive production. In Richmond, as was true in many cities across the country at the time, locomotives were not yet the sole offerings of a dedicated "locomotive shop" but rather largely experiments in diversification on the part of entrepreneurs such as Burr, those already established in proven crafts.

The Petersburg Railroad, the Montgomery Railroad, the Wilmington & Raleigh Railroad, and the Raleigh & Gaston Railroad were among Burr's customers, for which at least ten locomotives were manufactured from 1837

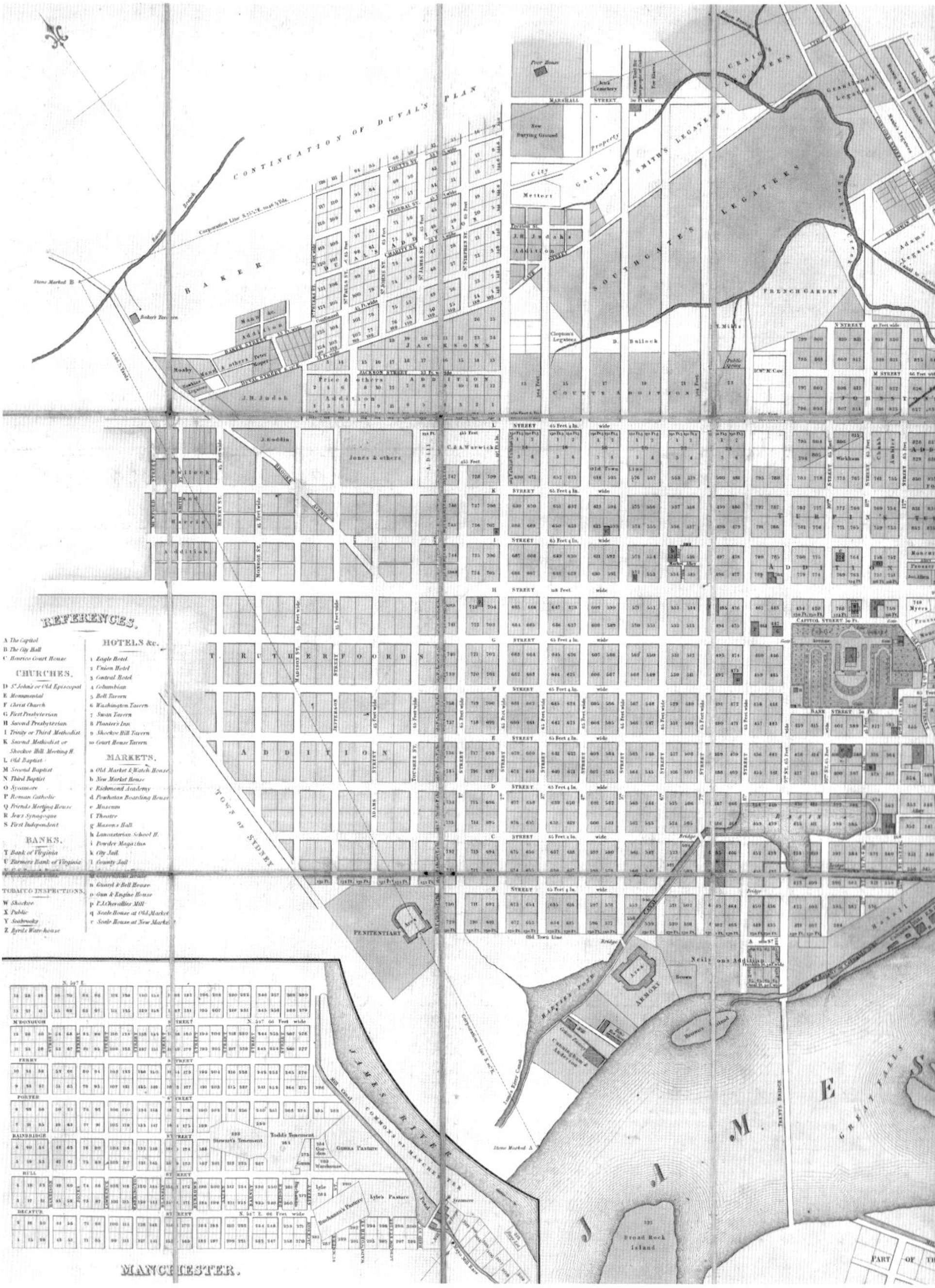

Plan of the City of Richmond, 1835, by Micajah Bates. *Albert and Shirley Small Special Collections Library, University of Virginia.*

MAP of the
PRIZE LOTS
of 100 Acres each in
BYRDS LOTTERY.
Sanders Island
JAMES RIVER
TOWN LAND
WATSONS Tenement
Westham Road
Scale of Feet
OLD TOWN
RICHMOND
COMMONS
RIVER
Part of Chesterfield Rail Road
COAL YARDS
HETH & RANDOLPH
MANCHESTER
SCALE of 400 FEET to 1 INCH.
Plan of the City of
RICHMOND
Drawn from Actual Survey and Original Plans
BY MICAJAH BATES,
1835.

to 1841, including four six-wheeled locomotives ordered on behalf of the Raleigh & Gaston in 1840.[26] Such engines would come to be classified as 4-2-0 locomotives in the Whyte notation system, meaning that the locomotives featured: four leading or carrying wheels (unpowered wheels that helped in guiding the engine along the track); two driving wheels (wheels powered by the engine, which actually propelled the locomotive); and no trailing wheels (which were used in some locomotives to further support the engine). This notational method, its use beginning in the early twentieth century, aided in describing vast numbers of locomotives of the steam era and was augmented further as locomotives themselves became larger and more complex.

According to the Raleigh & Gaston's chief engineer, Charles F.M. Garnett, the locomotive engines produced in Richmond were of superb quality. "The locomotives which we have received from Messrs. D. J. Burr, & Co. of Richmond, Virginia," Garnett reported to company stockholders in May 1840, "have fully answered our expectations. They are equal, if not superior, in beauty and strength of workmanship, and in performance, to any in this or any other country." The only issue Garnett apparently had was that, while of exceptional workmanship and functionality, the engines required two additional wheels be added, in order to reduce stress and damage to the road's wooden rails.[27] Burr also manufactured stationary engines for use in railroad repair shops, such as a five-horsepower low-pressure engine that powered lathes and other machinery for the RF&P, delivered in 1836.[28]

In 1843, Burr brought two partners into the firm, Thomas Sampson (in some records spelled Samson) and James Pae; the newly established Burr, Sampson & Pae continued to produce stationary engines and at least two additional locomotives, as well as an iron steamboat for use on the James River and Kanawha Canal in the hope that its speed of seven to eight miles per hour would "reduce freight, reduce the cost of travel—and more important than all…give a new impulse to the James River Canal and carry it to the Ohio River."[29] Sampson and Pae continued as the company's proprietors following Burr's retirement in 1849 and further diversified their offerings; they manufactured the machinery that helped hoist the equestrian statue of George Washington in Capitol Square in February 1858.[30]

The October 21, 1834 edition of the *Richmond Enquirer* carried a notice that a new enterprise, the Shockoe Manufacturing Company, had just completed work on a new machine shop and foundry. Located on D (later Cary) Street near Mayo's Bridge, the firm was prepared to take orders for threshing machines, mills, railroad fixtures, and steam engines.[31] David Burr's engine shop furnished the high-pressure, 15-horsepower stationary engine that powered the new endeavor.[32] On January 30, 1840, employee Charles Talbott signed an agreement with the owners of the company, transferring control of the firm to himself and his two brothers, James and Samuel, thereafter under the name of Talbott & Brothers. Following Samuel's death in January 1844, the firm was appropriately renamed Talbott & Brother.[33] Talbott played a significant role in nurturing a native population of ironworkers and engine machinists that would facilitate Richmond's accession as an industrial powerhouse by the beginning of the Civil War. The firm offered apprenticeships to young men to learn such skills as blacksmithing and finishing, for a period of several years, at a wage of $2.50 a week for their first year, increased by half a dollar each year until they reached the age of 21. At this point, they would be well suited to work for either Talbott himself or any of the other iron and engine works throughout the city.[34] Compared to other firms, Talbott & Brother's locomotive output was rather small, with only a few known to have been produced, including a 14-ton 4-4-0 locomotive named the *D. Anderson Jr* in 1849 and a 16-ton 4-4-0 named the *Louisa* in 1852, both purchased for use on the Louisa (later Virginia Central) Railroad, each with cylinders 12 x 18 inches, and 12 ½ x 20 inches, respectively.[35]

In 1835, Bavarian-born Peter Rahm immigrated to Richmond with his wife and several children in tow. One of his sons, Philip, at approximately 15 years of age, apprenticed as a blacksmith with Talbott & Brother. By no

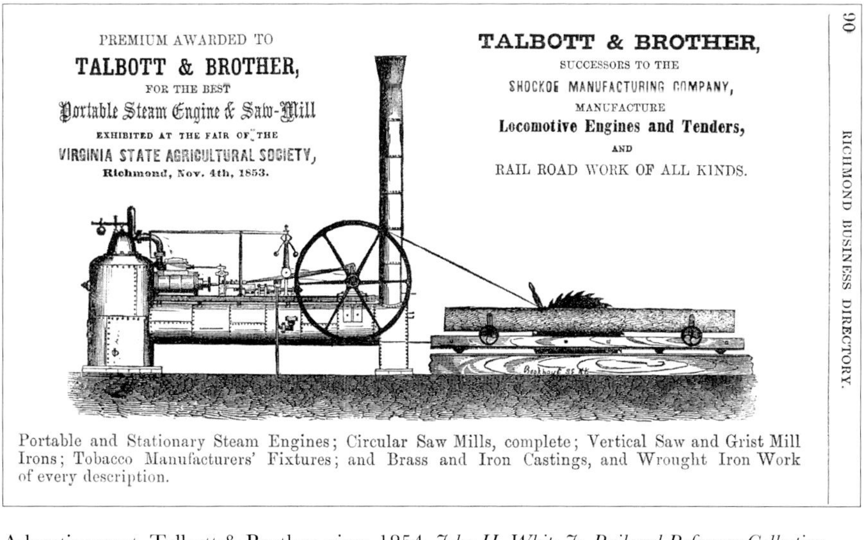

Advertisement, Talbott & Brother, circa 1854. *John H. White Jr. Railroad Reference Collection, Archives Center, National Museum of American History, Smithsonian Institution.*

later than 1849, Philip Rahm had established a small blacksmithing and tobacco mill shop, between 14th and 15th Streets, on the northern side of Cary Street; by March 1852, a new foundry and machine shop had been added, the entire enterprise now known as the Eagle Foundry.[36] Twenty-six workers were employed at the time of its founding, largely dedicated to manufacturing tools for Richmond's thriving tobacco industry, with a ten-horsepower engine, of Talbott & Brother design, powering the shop's machinery.[37] Rahm soon expanded his own portfolio to include stationary steam engines; by 1856, Rahm was advertising himself as a manufacturer of "locomotive engines, tenders, railroad cars, and all descriptions of railroad machinery," in addition to his standard offerings.[38] Rahm was nothing short of a mechanical and engineering prodigy, having garnered numerous awards and accolades from respected institutions for his work in designing and constructing highly efficient stationary engines and sawmills; however, despite his advertisements as a producer of locomotives, no evidence has yet been found to demonstrate that the Eagle Foundry manufactured a single locomotive.

On April 24, 1852, William S. Burr (relation, if any, to David Burr unknown) formed a partnership with one William Ettenger (often also spelled "Ettinger" in local papers), who had established, a few years earlier, a small iron and engine works, the Union Manufacturing Company, on Cary Street just next door to Talbott's Shockoe Manufacturing Company.[39] Burr & Ettenger produced stationary steam engines and circular saw mills, as well as both railcars and locomotives for surrounding railways. The firm, while relatively successful, was not without its mishaps; on July 10, 1853, Burr & Ettenger's works caught fire. The fire was contained largely to the pattern shop, which resulted in the loss of the entire shop and a sizable number of tools. However, the situation could have been far more dire, as the shop happened to border the City Gas Works, and the flames were so intense that the iron gates surrounding the Gas Works were later found to be "scorched and discolored."[40] For days and weeks to come, local newspapers harangued the fact that such a facility, so predisposed to conflagration, was allowed such proximity to the Gas Works, but no efforts were ever undertaken to remedy those concerns. During the 1850s, William Ettenger was a member of the board of managers of the Virginia Mechanics' Institute alongside Thomas Dodamead, the superintendent of the R&P, for which the firm produced at least one locomotive, the 4-4-0 *Henrico*, in 1852.[41] The *Henrico* performed admirably for a number of years until March 1856, when, while carrying mail and passengers along the R&P, one of its cylinders ruptured, requiring extensive repairs.[42] On May 13, 1857, the partnership of Burr and Ettenger was dissolved, and in its place Ettenger partnered with Horace P. Edmond to form a new venture, which seemingly redirected its focus to portable and stationary engines, railroads cars and "railroad fixtures of all kinds."[43] Ettenger & Edmonds made a name for themselves, and Richmond manufacturing, as several stationary engines they produced received widespread acclaim on account of their craftsmanship and efficiency, even within the pages of such respected periodicals as *Scientific American*. In July 1860, the firm was contracted to produce a steam-powered fire engine (at times also called a fire annihilator, or steam pumper), for use in Saint Petersburg, Russia, an engine so expertly crafted and reliable that "the Chief Engineer of the Richmond Fire Department [stated it was] worth the whole department put together at a fire."[44] The City of Richmond later ordered two duplicate engines for its own fire department.

Tredegar Locomotive Works

On February 27, 1837, two operations along the banks of the James River, the Virginia Foundry Company and the Tredegar Rolling Mills, merged to form the Tredegar Iron Works, under the supervision of one Francis B. Deane, a local merchant who was among the founding investors of the Virginia Foundry Company. The name Tredegar was bestowed in honor of Rhys Davies, the chief engineer at the works who had designed its rolling mills. Davies and a number of his colleagues hailed from the town of Tredegar and its eponymous iron works in Wales's Sirhowy River valley, a region long known and respected for the quality of both its iron works and collieries, as well as the caliber of the ironmasters and engineers it produced. The Sirhowy Valley also contained, among numerous other foundries, the Penydarren Ironworks of Merthyr Tydfil, which witnessed the trials of the first successful steam locomotive to run along rails in February 1804, the work of mechanical visionary Richard Trevithick.[45]

Iron ore mined in the western part of the state could easily be shipped downriver to Tredegar via the James River and Kanawha Canal, a portion of which ran directly behind the rolling mills, and coal from nearby Midlothian was easily accessible. From the beginning, however, Tredegar faced difficulties. Poor financial management on Deane's part was certainly an issue; more devastating was the economic panic and subsequent depression that gripped the nation in 1837. Securities restrictions in

European banking centers in 1836, the source of much of the investment that supported America's infrastructural growth, combined with the lack of a centralized banking authority following President Andrew Jackson's veto of the Second Bank of the United States' charter in 1832, provided impetus to the panic. European restraints were directly tied to the effects of the Deposit and Distribution Act of 1836, which required the federal government to redistribute surplus funds to the states, resulting in the movement of a significant amount of specie to western banks, at the expense of those in the East. Major banks on the East Coast saw their gold reserves dwindling, and bank runs unsurprisingly resulted. Banks across the nation shuttered, causing a severe depression that lasted until the early 1840s.[46] The chartering and construction of railroads was hindered for a time, and any firm supplying parts to railroads, such as Tredegar, suffered heavy losses. The closure of the James River and Kanawha Canal in 1838 due to repairs and expansions only deepened Tredegar's troubles, and Deane was soon replaced as president by local coal mine owner Nicholas Mills, who in turn was replaced by Joseph Reid Anderson of Botetourt County. Anderson, born in 1813, was a West Point graduate who, upon resigning his commission, helped oversee the construction of the Valley Turnpike, linking the towns of Winchester and Staunton in northern Virginia, before coming to Richmond, and Tredegar, initially to serve as the firm's sales agent, in 1841. Anderson leased the works in 1843 and took full ownership as proprietor in 1849.[47] It was under Anderson's guidance that Tredegar began to emerge from the panic years and cement itself among the nation's most prodigious iron works. Anderson, using his connections in the military, had begun to produce munitions and cannons for the U.S. Army as soon as he arrived at Tredegar, a market he continued to cultivate as proprietor. He also partitioned different divisions of Tredegar into separate entities, acquiring partners and aiming to strengthen each, in terms of both personnel and finances, with the ultimate goal of eventually recombining them back into a single, economically viable Tredegar.

By 1852, the Tredegar site had expanded into locomotive and other engine manufacturing operations, and to better suit the needs of a growing and constantly innovating industry, a new locomotive shop, three stories high, 150 by 50 feet, was constructed.[48] Just as Deane had reached abroad for workmen from Wales, so too did Anderson seek northern engineers to bolster his locomotive business. Respected engineers Daniel A. Pickering and John Souther of the Boston Locomotive Works traveled from Massachusetts to Richmond to join Anderson in 1852 to establish Anderson, Souther &

Joseph Reid Anderson, circa 1847. *Nathan Vernon Madison.*

Pickering. The partnership was not wholly successful, in either quality of products or finances; while the firm's products were initially lauded, a series of engine explosions soon overshadowed any early acclaim. An investigative committee composed of machinists and boilermakers concluded that poor workmanship and subpar iron were to blame for the explosion of the

Tredegar-made locomotive *Boubel* on August 18, 1853, which claimed the lives of three and injured several others. Following this report, the editors of the *American Railroad Journal* responded with a scathing indictment of both Tredegar engines and southern engineering as a whole:

> *The verdict of these men might be made to apply equally as well to the material used in other engines constructed at the Tredegar works. The reputation of the Tredegar iron, whatever it may once have been, would not warrant the use of such boiler plates as were liable to crack in bending, or to such rivet iron as would not withstand the working necessary to* [form] *a proper rivet head. We have seen the character and application of this iron to those locomotives and have often expressed fears of its failure. We are not in favor of establishing locomotive shops either in the south or west for the mere purpose of creating a market for materials not otherwise able to command a satisfactory sale.*[49]

Only six months into the following year, after the partnership with Souther and Pickering was dissolved, the locomotive division was already facing a $30,000 shortfall.[50] Tredegar's locomotive department was reorganized with several new partners, including a Scotsman whose family would later play an integral role in the founding of the Richmond Locomotive Works.

Matthew Delaney was born in 1815 in Dalbeattie, in southwestern Scotland along the coastline of the Solway Firth.[51] Not a great deal is known about his boyhood, aside from the fact that his father was named John; it is certainly possible that Matthew had some mechanical engineering experience as a teenaged apprentice, as Dalbeattie was home to a thriving granite industry. Matthew arrived in Massachusetts sometime in the mid-1840s, with his nephew Alexander. No later than 1847, Matthew relocated to Richmond, as he is recorded in that year as owner of at least two properties in Henrico, just outside Richmond and between Belvidere Street and the Tredegar Iron Works, and as holder of nearly $2,000 in personal property.[52] On April 12, 1849, he married Charity Lyman Clapp, originally of Connecticut and seven years his junior. As soon as he came to work at Tredegar, Delaney was already proving his acumen; in December 1851, the 4,000-pound, eight-wheeled locomotive *Lynchburg* was completed, one of several for the Virginia & Tennessee Railroad Company, which had as its eastern terminus the city of Lynchburg. Delaney designed and constructed the boilers for the engine, of which it was stated: "Every portion of the work and decoration of this superb engine reflects the greatest honor upon our Richmond artisans, and proves that the South may hereafter find within its own borders locomotives of the most superior kind."[53]

On July 1, 1854, Joseph R. Anderson and Matthew Delaney, along with Anderson's nephew Francis T. Glasgow (father of famed Richmond novelist Ellen Glasgow) and William Steptoe, became partners in Anderson, Delaney & Company, a firm dedicated primarily to engine production, both stationary and locomotive. Under the new partnership, of which Anderson was the senior partner and at times known as the Tredegar Engine Works or the Tredegar Locomotive Works, Delaney and Glasgow were entitled to a one-fifth's share in the company and Steptoe, one-tenth. As a partner, Delaney was entitled to a yearly salary of $1,500; Delaney's salary, if adjusted for inflation, would equal around $53,000 in 2022.[54] In 1854, the firm won contracts to manufacture two steam engines for the U.S. Navy steamer USS *Roanoke*. At this juncture, Anderson was heavily involved in naval orders, both at the locomotive shop as well as his foundry division, which was profiting handsomely thanks to contracts for shells, artillery, and naval guns. In January 1855, a locomotive produced by the partnership of Anderson and Delaney, *Amherst*, was praised for the strength and speed it demonstrated in hauling 75 head of cattle, thousands of bushels of wheat and various other items in 29 cars on the Southside Railroad, a route chartered in 1849 that connected City Point (now in modern-day Hopewell) just outside Petersburg to Lynchburg, some 120 miles to the west.[55] In 1856, the partnership of Anderson, Delaney & Company was dissolved as Anderson worked to consolidate his various enterprises. Delaney stayed on at Tredegar and gained an apprentice in his nephew Alexander. Between 1850 and 1860, approximately 70 locomotives were produced at Anderson's Tredegar Iron Works.[56] These included the *Augusta*, built in 1852 with cylinders 13 x 20 inches, the *Covington* (1853, 13 x 20 inches), the *Monroe* (1854, 14 x 20 inches), the *J.R. Anderson* (1854, 18 x 22 inches), the *Allegheny* (1856, 15 x 22 inches), and the *H.D. Whitcomb* (1856, 15 x 22 inches), all constructed for use on the Virginia Central Railroad.[57]

All of Matthew and Charity's children were born in Richmond, although only one, Chester Alexander (born June 22, 1852, and named in honor of Charity's father, Chester Clapp), survived to adulthood; son Lewis A., born on January 16, 1850, died 18 months later, and daughter Mary E. died almost a year to the day after her November 16, 1854 birth. The parents, unfortunately, did not live much longer than their two deceased children, as Charity died on April 23, 1855, with Matthew himself passing on a few years

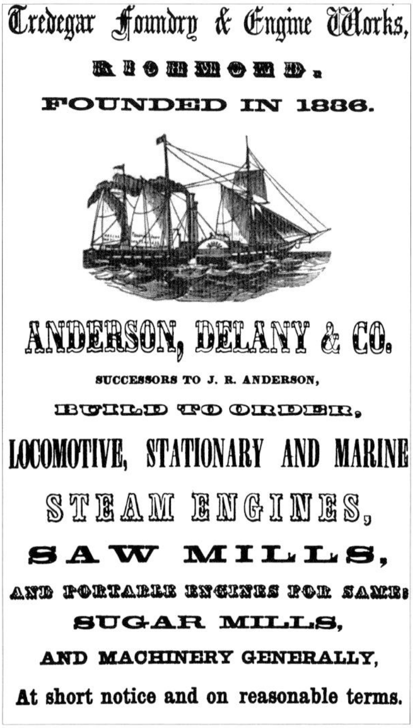

Advertisement, Anderson, Delaney & Co., 1854. *Statistical Gazetteer of the State of Virginia, 1854.*

before the onset of the Civil War, on August 6, 1858. Alexander was named as executor of his uncle's will, as well as legal guardian of Matthew's young son and heir, Chester Alexander.[58]

By the close of 1859, Joseph Reid Anderson had repurchased all interests in the various businesses operating at Tredegar, using capital from each venture to expand them individually before recombining them into a solitary Tredegar Iron Works; the business was augmented further by its absorption of the nearby Armory Rolling Mills, adjacent to the Virginia Manufactory of Arms and operated by Anderson's father-in-law, Dr. Robert Archer. By late 1860, locomotive production at Tredegar had ceased, due to several reasons.[59] Poor reception and orders for his locomotives, particularly following the *Bobuel* disaster, were likely. During the Panic of 1857, a hesitancy to extend credit, on which much capital machinery was ordered, was likely another.[60] The effects of European catastrophes ranging from poor harvests to the socialist revolutions of 1848 and the Crimean War (October 1853 to March 1856) seemed to coalesce at once to diminish foreign investment in America; stateside, a number of corruption and trading scandals plaguing Wall Street only compounded circumstances. The dual failures of N.H. Wolfe and Company, the oldest grain supplier in New York, and the Ohio Life Insurance and Trust Company, both in August 1857, were followed by multiple failures throughout the banking and railroad sectors, spawning an economic malaise that did not truly subside until the advent of the Civil War.[61] Anderson reasoned that perhaps after such industry-wide failures, placing greater emphasis on war materiel in the midst of rising regional tensions made greater pecuniary sense than expending capital and resources in the locomotive trade, a product line which, by that point, had not proven as successful as he had once hoped.

Locomotive production ceased in Richmond during the Civil War, with all major foundries, forges, and machine shops repurposed to support the war effort, with Tredegar becoming the principal supplier of cannon and ordnance to the Confederacy. Portable and stationary engines for use in sawmills, gristmills, and other commercial items were in production, as were rail spikes, chairs, and car wheels for the South's besieged railroads. As the war dragged on, an ever-increasing amount of material and manpower was sequestered for ordnance manufacture. In reply to a letter penned by the Memphis & Tennessee Railroad's treasurer C.F. Vance regarding locomotive orders, the Tredegar management replied, "We are so much engaged in defending the country that we can't stop to build Locomotives."[62] Even if within their power to do so, Tredegar's workmen had nowhere to renew engine production, a devastating fire in May 1863 having destroyed the former locomotive shop.[63]

Philip Rahm's Eagle Foundry, Talbott & Brother and Ettenger & Edmonds were also pressed into wartime manufacturing in one form or another, producing stationary engines, boat components, ordnance, and any other small items as requested; Sampson and Pae received several contracts to manufacture percussion caps for the Confederate army.[64] The Eagle Foundry suffered a tremendous loss in January 1862, when Philip Rahm was injured while aiding his workmen dislodging a mired wagon. He soon contracted lockjaw and passed away on January 10 at the age of 42. His son, Adolphus, then currently serving in the Confederate military, was released from service to manage the works in his father's stead.[65] As the Union army advanced, transportation of vital machinery and ore into the city ebbed, and the machinists' trade slowed to a trickle until ceasing completely just as the Confederacy was collapsing around them.

After the Fires

Forsaken, chaotic, and desolate are all apt descriptions of Richmond following the fall of the Confederacy in early April 1865. With Jefferson Davis having fled with his cabinet south to Danville on April 3, the remaining Confederate forces set fire to cotton and tobacco storehouses as well as any other buildings that could prove useful to the approaching Union army; a general conflagration soon commenced that resulted in the destruction of over 20 city blocks, almost the entirety of the city's downtown financial and industrial districts. The fire swept as far west as 4th Street, completely

Richmond, following the evacuation fires, April 1865, photograph by Alexander Gardner. *Library of Congress.*

obliterating the Virginia Manufactory of Arms in its wake, and as far north as Franklin Street, surrounding Capitol Square but sparing the Governor's Mansion and the Virginia Capitol due to their elevation atop Shockoe Hill. Nearly the entire area surrounding the James River and Kanawha Canal's Basin and south to the banks of the James was destroyed and as far eastward as Cary and 15th Street, either damaging or completely eradicating many of the city's engine and metalworking facilities. Almost as soon as they accepted Mayor Joseph Mayo's surrender of the city, Union forces worked to extinguish the numerous fires across Richmond. A city in complete ruins was soon inundated, as newly emancipated freedmen journeyed to Richmond from the countryside; as now-homeless White Richmonders within the city limits sought food and shelter; and as soldiers formerly loyal to the failed Confederacy returned home. The 10,000 Union soldiers stationed in the city provided for all as best they could while also simultaneously managing the rebuilding efforts.[66]

No fewer than 800 buildings were consumed in the evacuation fires, including all of the city's banks and a significant portion of restaurants, retailers, law offices, and numerous homes.[67] All of the prominent iron works and foundries along Cary Street—Rahm's Eagle Foundry, the works of Ettenger & Edmonds and Talbott's Shockoe Manufacturing Company—were completely destroyed in the fire. Joseph Anderson's Tredegar Iron Works, however, was preserved, partly due to it being far enough removed from the fire's path but also thanks to the efforts of workmen at the site in fending off any would-be arsonists and looters. Of the over 60 businesses affected by the fires to one degree or another, roughly 35 percent returned to operation within the next five years.[68] The Talbott brothers' works and

Richmond, following the evacuation fires, April 1865, photograph by Alexander Gardner. *Library of Congress.*

the Eagle Foundry were among those rebuilt, with Philip's son Adolphus assuming proprietorship of the latter; Ettenger & Edmonds relocated eastward toward Church Hill.

Traditional merchants and retailers along what was left of Main Street, many of which had relocated temporarily to Broad Street, were dependent on products shipped from outside the former capital of the Confederacy, which necessitated the reconstruction of Richmond's transportation infrastructure. Both the James River and its adjacent canal were congested with all manner of war debris and were largely unnavigable. The swiftest method of transportation for both resuming commerce and for troop movements if the need arose were the five railroads into Richmond, all of which were severely damaged in one form or another. The R&P, the Richmond & Danville, the RF&P and the Virginia Central had returned to some functional capacity by May 1865, with the Richmond & York River Railroad taking several more years, owing to the extensive damage it suffered in wartime. As rail service was restored, commerce recommenced, buoyed at times to above prewar levels owing in part to the reconstruction efforts throughout the city. In 1869, over 18 million pounds of freight were carried along the city's rail lines, a year that saw rail cargo in Baltimore, Norfolk, and Philadelphia combined dwarfed by that traveling through Richmond.[69] The Virginia Central underwent significant improvements, and new efforts were made to ensure it achieved the long-held dream of both canal and railroad builders in reaching the Ohio River; it was renamed the Chesapeake and Ohio Railroad (C&O) in 1868, and it did indeed reach the Ohio River in 1873.[70] As would be expected, several industries stood to profit from both the reconstruction of the region's rail network and the rebuilding efforts throughout the Burnt District, namely lumber, carpentry, and metalworking.

2

THE METROPOLITAN IRON WORKS / TANNER & DELANEY ENGINE COMPANY

1865–1887

For some, the evacuation fires cleared the slate to allow new ventures to arise, provided the capital and industrial acumen were present; this was certainly the case for three young men who, following their resignations from Tredegar, entered into business for themselves.

Delaney, Tanner and Ehbets

Alexander Delaney, nephew to Matthew, was born in Dalbeattie, Scotland, around 1830, and immigrated with his uncle to the United States in the mid-1840s; they stayed with relatives briefly in New England before relocating to Richmond.[71] Shortly after his naturalization as a U.S. citizen in Henrico County in 1851, Alexander joined his uncle at Tredegar, specifically in the engine and locomotive departments, eventually rising to the position of superintendent by 1861.[72] He left Tredegar to join the newly formed Confederate army but was soon removed from active service and ordered to return to his post at Tredegar, by order of Secretary of War Judah Benjamin, to aid in the industrial war effort. He did, however, serve as a first sergeant in the 6th Battalion, Virginia Infantry, commonly known as the Tredegar Battalion, a home guard composed largely of Tredegar employees. Though the unit was formerly believed to be open only to Tredegar workers, there exists some evidence that men from other establishments were allowed to join as well, as demonstrated by the presence in the battalion of George J.

Hooper Sr., a pattern maker employed at the nearby works of Sampson & Pae.[73] Both during and after the war, Alexander received high praise for his ability, in the face of dwindling resources and skilled workmen, to aid in the maintenance of Tredegar's production levels.[74]

William Elam Tanner, son of Tredegar partner John F. Tanner and Harriet L. Tanner, was born in New Canton, Buckingham County, on March 13, 1836.[75] As a young man, William Tanner joined his father at Tredegar as the firm's bookkeeper; in 1863, Tanner resigned his position to serve in the Confederate army. Following the Second Battle of Manassas, the Confederate government requested his return to Tredegar, as its shell and ordnance production was vital to the war effort. Like Delaney and many other Tredegar employees, William Tanner joined the Tredegar Battalion and commanded the unit for some time until war's end. Over the course of the war, Tanner attained the rank of colonel, an appellation he would carry the remainder of his life.[76]

A native of the German Confederation and the son of a Hamburg state architect, Jacob Otto Ehbets was born on September 26, 1836, one of nine children. Jacob received a high degree of education both inside and out of the classroom, working first in several machine shops before earning a degree in engineering from what is today the Karlsruhe Institute of Technology in Baden, Germany.[77] In 1857, Jacob, along with his brother Charles, immigrated to America, first to New York. While Charles remained in the North, becoming a civil engineer in Hartford, Connecticut, Jacob traveled south to Richmond. Immediately, his mechanical aptitude and education led him to Tredegar, where he aided in the firm's cannon production shortly before the war began. Like many Germans who settled in Richmond, Ehbets was Lutheran, but according to one contemporary source, "he might properly be called a liberal or free-thinker."[78] During the Civil War, he worked alongside Canadian Uri Haskins in overseeing the rolling of the iron plating for the former *Merrimack*, rechristened the CSS *Virginia*. Jacob was also a member of the Tredegar Battalion, and it is not unreasonable to assume that he was one of the battalion members who protected Tredegar from complete destruction during the fires of April 1865.

This trio of former Tredegar employees joined together, amid the ruins of a devastated city, to form a new venture: the Metropolitan Iron Works. Tanner's connections to Tredegar, as well as his status as a scion of a wealthy family, provided the new venture with needed capital and public name recognition; he was personally connected to many of Richmond's elites as well, having been made a Freemason in April 1858, and had risen to the

'. E. TANNER. ALEX. DELANY.

METROPOLITAN WORKS,

CANAL STREET, FROM 6TH TO 7TH, RICHMOND, VA.

(OFFICE, NO. 110, 7TH STREET.)

WM. E. TANNER & CO.

STATIONARY AND PORTABLE ENGINES, SAW MILLS, BARK, GRIST AND PLASTER MILLS, AND MILL GEARING,

Bolts and Castings for bridges, Iron and Brass Work, Passenger Platform and Box Cars, improved Tobacco and other Machinery of all kinds, built and repaired.

OUR ENGINES TOOK FIRST PREMIUM AT THE GREAT STATE FAIR HELD AT MACON, GA., NOV. 16, 1869, OVER ALL COMPETITORS.

Read the following Report of the Special Committee on Machinery, at the Virginia State Fair, at Richmond, in November, 1869:

W. E. TANNER & Co., Richmond, Va., exhibit a twenty-five horse power Portable Engine, prepared expressly for driving the Machinery on exhibition.

This engine is well adapted to any purpose to which it may be applied, either in the ordinary agricultural operation, or in driving of Saw or Grist Mills and can be made of any size or power required. For its merits *as the best piece of machinery* on the grounds and its economy of operation, we recommend a FIRST CLASS PREMIUM.

Respectfully submitted,
FRANK KAHL,
CHAS. CAMPBELL,
JAMES L. DAVIS,
C. BRADLEY.
} Committee.

Advertisement, Metropolitan Iron Works, from *Evening News*, April 29, 1870.

rank of Master Mason within a month's time. Business, family, and societal networks, as well as the financial security these associations made possible, ensured that he was made the senior partner of the firm. Correspondences uncovered by locomotive historian John H. White Jr. in the 1970s attest to the fact that, apparently in response to the inquires of a curious investor, "Tanner's father is rich, and will no doubt back [the venture] if necessary."[79] Likewise, it was understood that "Delaney…is a man of very modest means and no property—does not improve the firm pecuniarily but is a thorough business man and would add strength in the way of mechanical genius, patronage, etc."[80] Obviously, the workload between the partners was distributed according to their natural strengths; Delaney and Ehbets were largely responsible for the mechanical and engineering prowess needed to successfully operate such an establishment, while Tanner was the understood manager of the firm, as well as its "public face."

All manner of iron and brass castings, railroad axles and wheels, and iron bars and grates for homes and storefronts were among Metropolitan's initial offerings, and the firm soon established itself as a trusted producer of machinery for the city's various enterprises. During the first week of February 1869, Metropolitan was busily constructing a new steam boiler for Charles Y. Morriss's Virginia Steam Sugar Refinery at Rocketts, its predecessor having exploded earlier in the week.[81] Much of the company's early success was owed to the iron it produced for the ongoing rebuilding and reconstruction of war-damaged railroad bridges in Richmond, as well as throughout Virginia and surrounding states.[82] The enterprise, located between 6th and 7th on the northern side of Canal Street in a small brick building only a short distance from Tredegar, operated a foundry for castings as well as wood, sash, machine, and blacksmith shops. No blast or puddling furnaces are mentioned in any of Metropolitan's circulars, which makes it quite likely, owing to the closeness (both personally and geographically) that the trio still maintained with their former employer, that much of the iron or copper needed for orders was purchased from Tredegar; scrap iron, brass, and copper were also procured by the firm for recycling and repurposing.[83]

The years 1869 and 1870 were busy for Metropolitan Iron Works, in terms of personnel as well as physical growth. By mid-1869, Alexander Delaney had become a senior partner in the Metropolitan Iron Works, which by that point was alternatively also known as Tanner, Ehbets & Delaney; in July 1869, Ehbets resigned from the firm following Tanner's purchase of the former's interest in the company, now referred to in circulars as the Metropolitan Iron Works as well as William E. Tanner & Co., interchangeably. In terms of physical space, the firm continued to grow; by September 1870, it occupied the entire city block bounded by 6th and 7th and Cary and Canal, which allowed space for several new iron and brass foundries, as well as additional forges for the blacksmith shop. Metropolitan had expanded to such a degree that it now required space outside of its single-block confines; the former home of James Pae (of Sampson & Pae), located nearby on 6th, was used entirely for pattern storage by the company.[84]

Ehbets seemingly had nothing but praise for Richmond and his former partners, writing a brief address to readers of the August 2, 1869 edition of Richmond's *Daily Dispatch:* "In retiring from the firm of Tanner, Ehbets, & Delaney, I desire to return my thanks to the public for the kind encouragement and patronage extended to us, and solicit a continuance of the same to the new house."[85] Ehbet's life after leaving Richmond, however, was far from a retirement. He first went to work as an engineer for the American Bridge Company of Chicago for several years. In 1874, Ehbets relocated to Milwaukee to serve in the employ of the Milwaukee Bridge Company, before moving on again, in 1878, to design engines used in municipal waterworks for the E.P. Allis Company, also of Milwaukee. Jacob and his wife, Lemira (born December 1, 1834), had only one child, a daughter named Virginia Pauline, born on June 8, 1880.[86] The Milwaukee, Lake Shore & Western Railroad hired Ehbets in 1884 to act as engineer on the railway's bridges. In 1893, he relocated yet again to the Wisconsin Central Railway, designing and overseeing the construction of several new railroad bridges.[87] Lemira and Jacob spent the remaining years of their lives in Milwaukee, passing away on March 18, 1908, and February 16, 1923, respectively.[88]

Back in Richmond, in early January 1871, a new partner, Virginius Newton, was inducted into the company's ranks. Newton, a native of Norfolk born on October 27, 1844, traced his family's origins to the era of the House of Burgesses and likewise belonged to several genealogical organizations, including the Sons of the American Revolution. While serving in the Confederate navy, Newton was present for the March 1862 battle between the USS *Monitor* and the CSS *Virginia* at Hampton Roads.[89] Newton's presence at the Metropolitan Works was perhaps something of an internship and introduction to the monied interests in Richmond; by 1873, Newton was dividing his efforts between the Works and a new position at the prestigious Davenport & Co., an insurance and investment firm founded in 1863, whose cofounder Isaac Davenport Jr. happened to be Newton's father-in-law. Newton did not stay with Tanner for long; as of February 16, 1876, he resigned his position at the Works to establish a wholesale

Virginius Newton. *From* Richmond Virginia: The City on the James, *1903.*

groceries business. Newton would continue in Richmond's business circles, most notably as president of the First National Bank of Richmond, a position previously held by the aforementioned Davenport Jr. and one that his former employer Tanner, who spoke highly of Newton in subsequent years, could likely depend on for friendly relations.[90]

Within only five years of its founding, the Metropolitan Iron Works had become a recognized innovator in the manufacture of stationary steam engines, winning acclaim for two 45-horsepower steam engines displayed at the Georgia and Virginia State Fairs in 1868 and 1869, respectively.[91] By 1870, the new facility employed approximately 135 hands, on shifts that ran both day and night.[92] In 1872, the partners patented a new steam water vacuum gauge that sounded an alarm when steam in the boiler reached a certain pressure, thereby allowing the operator to open a safety valve and avoid a potential explosion; orders for Tanner's boilers and stationary engine were being placed from as far away as Texas.[93]

Tanner and Delaney were also successfully competing against other Richmond foundries for lucrative municipal contracts; one such bid, to furnish a gas holder for the Richmond City Gas Works, caused something of a stir within the Richmond iron industry.[94] After it was announced in March 1871 that the contract for the new holder was awarded to Messrs. Tanner & Co., the Tredegar Company and Charles Talbott jointly issued a formal complaint, as well as an open letter in city newspapers, accusing Tanner, and the Richmond City Council itself, of nothing less than collusion. The accusation, signed by Tredegar's Joseph Reid Anderson, his son Archer Anderson, Robert S. Archer, and Francis Glasgow, claimed that Tredegar's bid of $36,950 was unfairly dismissed in favor of Tanner's $47,000 bid and that councilmen worked with Tanner, for reasons unknown, to ensure his firm, and not Tredegar, Talbott, or any of the other bidders, received just consideration. The city council replied in its own open letter, justifying the decision, and Delaney supplied a detailed, technical explanation as to why his firm's designs for a 12-columned holder as opposed to Tredegar's 8 columns were, from an engineering standpoint, more practical, even if

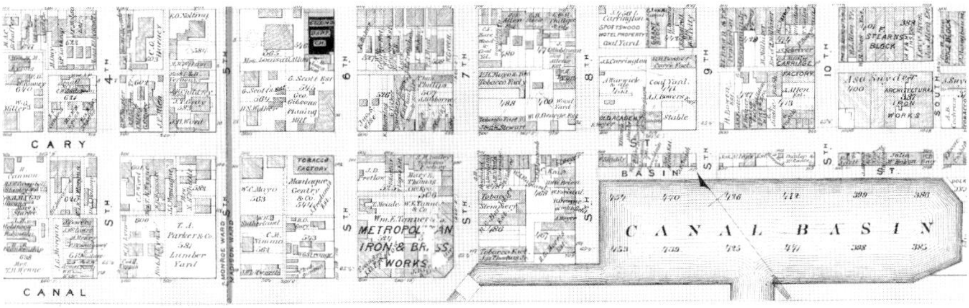

Metropolitan Iron Works, at 7th and Canal, *Illustrated Atlas of Richmond*, F.W. Beers, 1877. *Library of Congress.*

costlier. Tanner issued a public reply several days later to his former mentors, stating that "as a matter of *reputation*, which as young men and manufacturers, we are anxious to build up, we would not part with our contract for double what we expect to make out of it; and the *Tredegar company* can't buy it *at any price*." The contract did indeed remain with Tanner & Co., for in June of the following year, the new holder was finished and put into service.[95] This brief scuffle, however, did not sour relations between Tredegar and Tanner, as the two companies continued favorable dealings with each other and even collaborated on some future endeavors.

The firm remained a frequent contractor to the municipal sector for years to come, in both Richmond and beyond. In May 1883, Tanner & Co. was awarded a $5,000 contract to upgrade the city's gas works; two months later, a similar bond was granted on behalf of the municipal gas works of New Castle, Pennsylvania.[96] On December 3, 1884, the company hosted an elaborate, catered ceremony observing the completion of its latest contract, a massive overhauling of the Richmond Gas Works, including new condensers, scrubbers, and various other pieces of machinery. The condensers, which aided in purifying the gas from incinerated coal, were capable of handling one million cubic feet per day; the scrubber, a large tank of water through which gas was further purified before storage and eventual citywide distribution, was 42 feet high and 6 feet in circumference. The fabrication of all machinery was overseen personally by both Alexander Delaney and assistant engineer William Simpkin and was part of a municipal contract valued at $15,000.[97] In January 1885, the firm was the winning bidder, against nine competitors, on a $10,000 contract to fabricate four Lancashire boilers for use at the newly renovated Nashville, Tennessee waterworks.[98] Later in 1885, the company was awarded the full construction contract for new gas works in Knoxville, Tennessee.[99] Metropolitan-built stationary and portable engines were frequent exhibits at state fairs and industrial expositions throughout the South, usually claiming first prize against those of its rivals.

By 1873, the firm had expanded its operation to include more complicated products, such as turbines; it also began acting as the local retail agent for several northern firms, including Pennsylvania's N.F. Burnham turbine company, which supplied turbines across the nation, from the lauded factories in Lowell, Massachusetts, to the raceways at nearby Tredegar.[100]

In the late 1870s, the Metropolitan Iron Works opened a new phase of its business, one for which it, and its successors' futures, would be based on: locomotive engines. Given the limited size of the Canal Street site, mainline locomotives were not feasible for the time being; however, smaller engines, made to run on city tramways and other narrow-gauge lines, as well as some industrial railways, were certainly viable and offered an "in-road" into the locomotive industry. In June 1877, the company completed the *Ellie Parker*, a narrow-gauge locomotive built for use on the Forest Grove Tramway, a wooden rail line used to carry lumber from sawmills in nearby Goochland County to the Richmond docks. The customer was obviously quite pleased with the quality of the product, as he wrote in August 1878 to the company:

> *Gentlemen—the Locomotive, "Ellie Parker," purchased from you twelve months ago, 7 x 14 cylinder, 3 feet gauge, has performed to our entire satisfaction in every particular, pulling dead weight against grades ranging from 100 to 700 feet to the mile, making three trips of sixty miles per day, and doing it all* with ease *fully as well as any locomotive on regular railroads. In a word, we challenge the country to furnish an engine that will do as much and as heavy work for its weight and inches, as we are compelled, from the natural hilliness of the country to do with this. Wishing you the abundant success that the merits of your work deserve.*[101]

The *Daily Dispatch*'s contention that this was "the first locomotive constructed here [in Richmond] since the war" is certainly plausible. While there are several accounts of locomotive engines being assembled in Richmond after the Civil War, such as the engine *Fredericksburg* at the RF&P depot in March 1866, it is uncertain if these were fully constructed in Richmond or instead fabricated elsewhere and simply reassembled there.[102] There seems to be no indication of any locomotive engine manufactured by Tanner and Delaney's shops prior; thus, for all intents and purposes, and until

Right: Hitching post, manufactured by the Metropolitan Iron Works, Clay Street, Richmond, Virginia, 2022. *Nathan Vernon Madison.*

Below: Hitching post, manufactured by the Metropolitan Iron Works, Clay Street, Richmond, Virginia, 2022. *Nathan Vernon Madison.*

evidence surfaces otherwise, the *Ellie Parker* holds not only the distinction of returning, at the very least continuous and sustained, locomotive production to Richmond but also the honor of laying the foundations for what would become a behemoth of Virginia industry.

As would be expected of one of Richmond's societal elites, William Tanner became active in Richmond political and societal affairs. Briefly during the 1870s, he served as a Virginia state senator, representing Richmond and Henrico residents in the 7th Senate District, and in 1875 became one of several vocal proponents of reinvigorating the region's coal and canal businesses. Tanner and other Richmond businessmen argued in favor of importing coal from the Kanawha region of West Virginia along the C&O to Buchanan, Virginia, where it would then be shipped downriver via the James River and Kanawha Canal to Richmond. Tanner considered "the coke from this coal equal to the anthracite coal, ton for ton, in the manufacture of iron." Despite Tanner's best efforts, and other prominent Richmond businessmen lending their ardent support, the plan never gained traction beyond discussions.[103] In 1878, the Richmond & Alleghany Railroad was chartered and began laying rails along the James River and Kanawha Canal's towpath, hastening the waterway's slow demise until its use ended entirely; the Richmond & Alleghany was eventually incorporated into the C&O.[104]

Brought about first by failures in European stock markets and the subsequent failure of many New York financing firms, most notably Jay Cooke & Co., the Panic of 1873 affected railroads particularly so, as they had spent years expanding their lines, buoyed by easy money from financiers and often building railroads from which no real profit could be reaped. As in 1857, companies supplying railroad accoutrements faced severe hardships and at times outright collapse, with Tredegar itself entering receivership for several years. However, there is no extant evidence that the events of 1873 injured the Metropolitan Iron Works to any significant degree, likely simply due to the fact that the mainline railroad industry, dealt a particularly heavy blow by the panic, was not among Tanner and Delaney's primary customers. In the years following the Panic of 1873, William Tanner, in agreement with many southern businessmen of the time, saw it as another folly of federal government and its reliance on greenbacks, the value of which could easily fluctuate. When asked, in 1875, his thoughts on the debate regarding the resumption of specie payments in the panic's aftermath, Tanner remarked:

> *I am opposed to inflation. Enlargement only makes a dollar worthless, and the wages of the workingmen will not purchase an equal amount in proportion to the depreciation of its value. If there was twice as much currency its purchasing power would be greatly diminished, while wages would be little, if any increased. The working of inflation during the Confederacy was a fair example of its evils....Personally I am inclined to specie-payments, but am not certain of its effects on the country.*[105]

After his brief sojourn into elected office, Tanner soon refocused his energy on the Metropolitan Iron Works, with local newspapers ready to heap praise upon his endeavor, hailed as just one of several harbingers indicating Richmond's, and Virginia's, reemergence as an industrial force.

> *Messrs. William E. Tanner & Co. report that they are crowded with work. The Colonel has laid aside his senatorial toga, and is deeply immersed in the question how to supply their orders for stationary engines. He was found yesterday "talking steam-engine" to a Southside gentleman more earnestly than ever he discussed politics; and in consequence, his partner, Mr. Newton, had to submit to reportorial questioning. For weeks orders have been rushing in upon them, until they have not only had to increase their force, but in some departments work over hours. Business is indeed very brisk with them.*[106]

On November 11, 1881, an enormous blaze struck the Works, originating on the second floor of a shop at the corner of 7th and Canal and spreading throughout the facility into several adjacent buildings, destroying much of the firm's tools, machinery, and casting patterns. The entire loss was estimated to be at least $90,000. Generously, several other iron works in the area, including Tredegar, offered Tanner & Co. the use of their facilities for the completion of any orders delayed by the fire until the damaged buildings were restored.[107] The fire struck at a particularly unfortunate time, as the company was at the height of its business, employing around 250 workers and engaged in the construction of 100 engines of varying size and purpose.[108] Tanner and associates were able to rebuild the Works, only for it to be nearly destroyed yet again the following March, its survival owed largely to the efforts of the workmen and neighbors who rushed to suppress the flames, heartfelt appreciation for which Tanner made known in an open letter published in the city papers.[109]

Tanner & Delaney Engine Company

These two fires, however, spoke to serious deficiencies regarding the Metropolitan Iron Works premises. On a crowded street, a stone's throw away from the Tredegar Iron Works, the site at 7th and Canal was so compact that any small spark could theoretically destroy the entire facility, if not several city blocks. Further, the site was not conducive to potential growth, particularly if the partners hoped to enter into mainline locomotive production. Even as the facilities were undergoing repairs, Tanner and Delaney sought a location that would allow for this desired expansion and found it on a 25-acre plot in Shockoe Valley, on the northern end of 7th Street, roughly one mile northwest of Capitol Square and outside the city limits in Henrico County, purchased from Richmond industrial and financial magnate James H. Dooley.

Construction of this new plant began in late 1881, while production of boilers, sawmills, gristmills, gas works apparatus, light locomotives (similar to the *Ellie Parker*), and other machinery continued on at the original plant for several more years; it was during the construction of this new facility, on March 7, 1882, that the Metropolitan Iron Works was recognized by the State of Virginia as having changed its name to the Tanner & Delaney Engine Company, with a new initial capital stock of $300,000.[110] Colonel William E. Tanner was named president of the new firm and Alexander Delaney appointed superintendent. By July 1882, the Canal site was posted for sale, in anticipation of operations moving to the new facility by that following January, although work was not completed and the company relocated until the summer of 1883.[111] The original Canal foundry and shops of the Metropolitan Iron Works were soon purchased and expanded by tobacconists P.H. Mayo and Bros.[112] By 1886, tobacco producers Allen & Ginter., T.C. Williams & Co., and P.H. Mayo & Bros. Stemmery, as well as Valentine's Meat Juice Works, all operated manufacturing and storage facilities on that block.

The new Tanner & Delaney Engine Company shops were a vast improvement when compared to the firm's previous dwellings and truly brought it in line with the rest of the locomotive manufacturing industry at the time—a large facility built specifically with locomotive production in mind. The transition from the old facility to the new was also symbolic of a change ongoing throughout American industry. Much of America's manufacturing architecture had its origins in the simple mills and forges that were prerequisites for any small town or village in the colonial and early republic eras. Men were expected to understand the building of such valuable structures, and that widespread knowledge led to many of America's earliest industrial structures being built along those examples.[113] Richmond's own early history of locomotive construction demonstrates this quite clearly; Burr, Sampson, Talbott, and Anderson did not construct their locomotives in what, in 1885, would have been recognized by professional standards as "locomotive works" but rather buildings built to more general, longstanding designs, within which such new industries were carried on as best they could be. As industry advanced, and the needs of mechanization and automation were taken into ever greater account, industrial architecture underwent augmentation as well. Manufactories were progressively designed to meet the needs of the particular industry for which they were intended, and the new industrial architects and engineers who were cultivated as a result came to be highly valued experts—so much so that, in time, the historical flow of technology was reversed and Americans began traveling to Europe to design factories there.[114] Structures were increasingly influenced by the work being carried out in them, which in turn was constantly evolving as manufacturing processes themselves evolved, the change in structural form between a building that relied on belts and pulleys for power and one using steam or electric power being a prime example.[115] Such increased emphasis on the melding of form and function allowed for greater architectural freedom

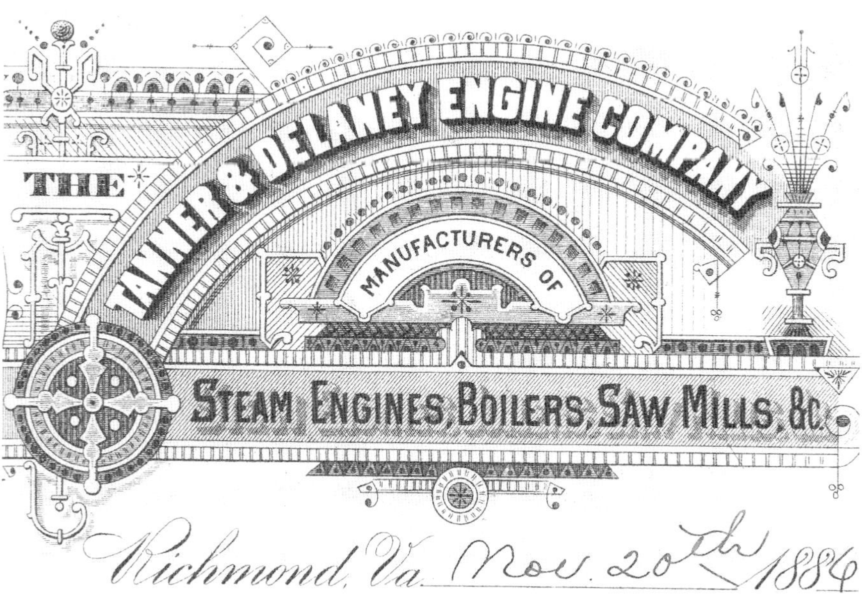

Letterhead, Tanner & Delaney Engine Company, 1886. *Nathan Vernon Madison.*

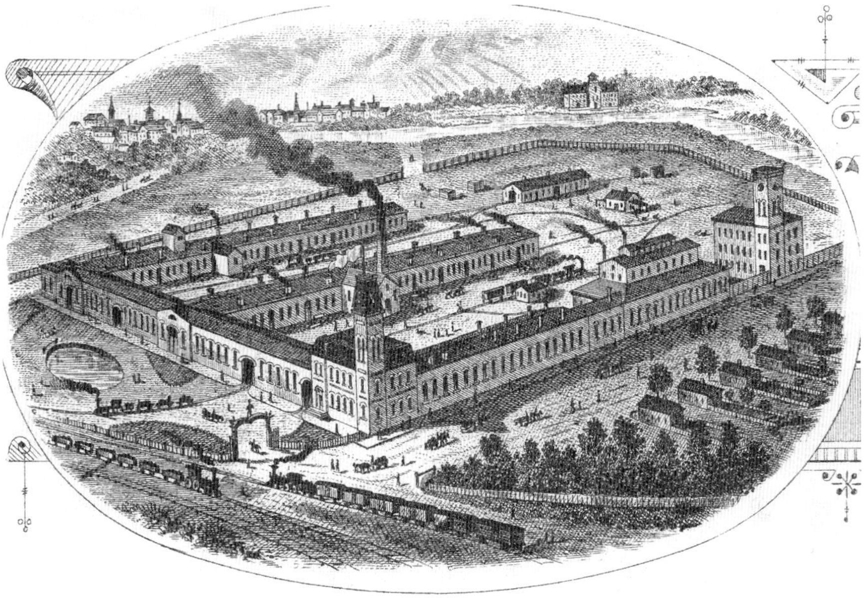

Letterhead, Tanner & Delaney Engine Company, 1886. *Nathan Vernon Madison.*

and the construction of the enormous, sprawling works that defined the late nineteenth- and early twentieth-century industrial landscape.

Although mainline locomotives were not yet being produced, the new Tanner & Delaney plant, 12 acres in total, leaving 13 acres open for expansion if need be, was obviously constructed with the intention of doing so in mind, as the facility matched other mainline locomotive shops across the country. The plant was in the form of a backward-facing *E*, with the three "prongs" of the *E*, or wings as they could be called, housing a 66-by-140-foot blacksmith shop attached to a 69-by-56-foot pattern shop; a machine shop, 196 by 96 feet; and a boiler shop, 196 by 66 feet, from north to south. The spine of the complex, connecting all three wings and bordering what would later become an extension of 7th Street, was the firm's 300-by-43-foot erecting shop. Along the northern edge of the plant was a 150-by-200-foot iron foundry housing several cupola furnaces and core ovens for producing patterns, which were stored in a building to the foundry's west; connecting the iron foundry and blacksmith shop was a small brass foundry, 41 by 56 feet. Directly south of the foundry and laterally in line with the machine shop was the firm's carpenter's shop. The company's public office and main entrance were in the upper northeast corner of the complex, between the pattern and erecting shops.[116] Even after the advent of electric lights, tradition dictated that shops make as much use of natural lighting as possible, resulting in the large, open windows ubiquitous to many manufactories of the era.

Newspapers throughout the state were eager to sing the praises of the new and improved site:

> *From the first location, which had not area sufficient for enlarged designs, they put their plant on twelve acres of land on the Chesapeake and Ohio Railway near the limits of the City, and there is now to be found perhaps the largest and best equipped Engine-works in the United States.... They are in the form of a hollow square with three sides. The front handsomely ornamented with running water, lakes, shrubbery, and flowers. If all the shops which are systematically placed in the general plan were in one line the frontage would be nearly two thousand feet. A water tank, holding 25,000 gallons, is on the summit of a tower 100 feet high. The buildings are all brick and of stylish architectural designs. The water serves for protection against fire as well as for other purposes. Railroad tracks connecting with the Chesapeake and Ohio line run through all the shops and grounds.*[117]

Tanner & Delaney soon made further forays into the light locomotive field, still not prepared to enter mainline production as of yet. Following previous success in the late 1870s with engines for industrial or intracity rails, the firm inaugurated a new product line—pole road locomotives. Pole road locomotives were a growing necessity throughout America's lumber industry, particularly in the South. Natural waterways and man-made canals were the primary routes by which loggers sent timber downstream for processing, oftentimes aided by natural flooding. However, as floods did not occur at regular intervals and beasts of burden proved less than ideal in such environments, other means of transportation were essential. Solutions arrived first in the form of tramways of wooden rails and ties, and later with pole roads—simpler tracks consisting of trees, shorn of their limbs, laid to create paths and lacking crossties of any sort.[118]

Such easily constructed railways were also less permanent than traditional rails and could be adjusted or removed entirely, per the needs of the loggers.

The first patent for a locomotive to run on these pole roads, with wheels not flanged like traditional locomotives but rather slightly grooved in order to ride atop the poles, belonged to former Union officer Edward P. Cowles.[119] While Cowles's engine proved a tad too complicated for the needs and rigors of the lumber industry, a more streamlined variation sprang from the mind of Alabama inventor and gristmill owner William Edward Cole. Cole's engine, first produced at Alabama's Montgomery Iron Works in the summer of 1883, featured several advancements on Cowles's original, such as a design that ensured the boiler remained upright and stable, even on the roughest of terrains. The pole road engine's use of individually driven wheels with their own chains, which ensured the engine still operated even if one chain was disabled, as well as the size and shape of the wheels, proved most beneficial for the engine's expected workload.[120]

In August 1885, Alexander Delaney traveled to Montgomery to inspect Cole's engines, and within a month, an agreement to produce Cole pole road locomotives was inked. Cole traveled to Richmond to help oversee the production of his design, and by the end of April 1886, a Cole pole road locomotive produced by Tanner & Delaney was performing test runs before potential customers. Advertisements Tanner & Delaney placed in industry journals touted the features and qualities of the pole road engine:

> *Pole Road Locomotives, of the pattern constructed by us are the only ones that are of any practical value, or designed on proper principles for the work in which they are to be employed. They are built under an arrangement with the patentee, W.E. Cole....The boiler is made of the best selected homogeneous steel plates, and is thoroughly tested to carry a high pressure. The frame work is of wrought iron and steel, and is very substantial and heavy. The driving wheels are thirty inches diameter on the tread, and are massive and strong. The wheels are each driven separately by a chain having a breaking strain of over twelve tons....The Engine Shaft, Master Shaft, and Axles are all of the best steel. The Axles are mounted on a double spiral spring, and are so arranged in the axle-box bearings that they can be adjusted for any stretching in the chain. A first-class Governor controls the speed of the Engine, which is about five.*[121]

As historians Mike McKnight and Robert T. Rhode have described in their expertly researched history of the Cole pole road engines, several of the Tanner & Delaney models show marked differences from those produced by others. Cylinder cocks, minute ports common in most engines of the time that aided in removing condensation from the cylinders (which aids in engine efficiency and helps prevent potential damage when steam is introduced during operation), were lacking from the Tanner & Delaney models; while this was advertised as a benefit, it is possible that this was the result of a small firm attempting to make a name for itself in

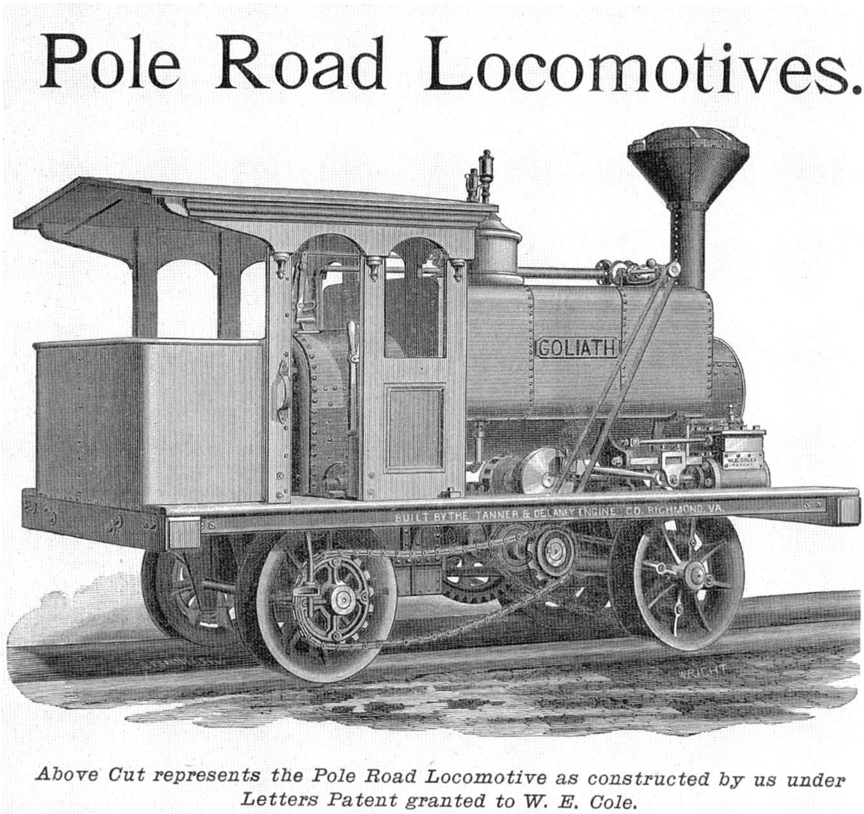

Advertisement, Tanner & Delaney Pole Road Locomotive, 1885. *John H. White Jr. Railroad Reference Collection, Archives Center, National Museum of American History, Smithsonian Institution.*

a crowded field by offering an engine that cost slightly less to produce.[122] Further, the presence of a governor, used to regulate the speed of the engine, was by that point a rarity in American locomotives. The firm's lumber-related accessories, such as pole road engines, timber cars, and other accoutrements, proved quite popular, selling well both nationally and internationally, aiding in a growing name recognition that would bode well for the company in later years.

In addition to pole road locomotives, Tanner & Delaney continued to offer other narrow-gauge engines for city and industrial use. The firm produced, among other varieties, smaller locomotives that counted four driving wheels, 26 inches in diameter and 7 inches wide, and two leading wheels, as well as a trailing truck with four 18-inch-diameter wheels; available in range

Tanner & Delaney Pole Road Locomotive, date unknown. *John H. White, Jr. Railroad Reference Collection, Archives Center, National Museum of American History, Smithsonian Institution.*

from three- to five-foot gauge, these engines were able to haul upward of 30 tons on wooden rails and 60 tons on rails made of iron.[123] Customers were highly pleased with Tanner & Delaney products, if testimonials are to be taken into account. "Concerning the Locomotive bought of you, we never tested its full capacity. We only know that it worked nicely, and was never out of order during the time we ran it," wrote J.W. Beasley, president of the "F.L." (most likely Fort Leavenworth) Railroad, in June 1886. "We had two first-class engineers in charge of it at different times, and both of them said they never saw a better locomotive. We never felt the slightest dissatisfaction towards it."[124] Stationary and portable engines, steam boilers, and municipal equipment continued to round out the company's catalogue.

Despite its seeming success, Tanner & Delaney was facing dire financial straits. The overhead costs of erecting and operating the newly built plant apparently far outweighed the revenue the Works reaped; the company owed significant sums to creditors and was unable to even make interest payments on the facility's mortgage as early as 1886.[125] Investors came to the rescue and saved the company from dissolution, but William Tanner, as

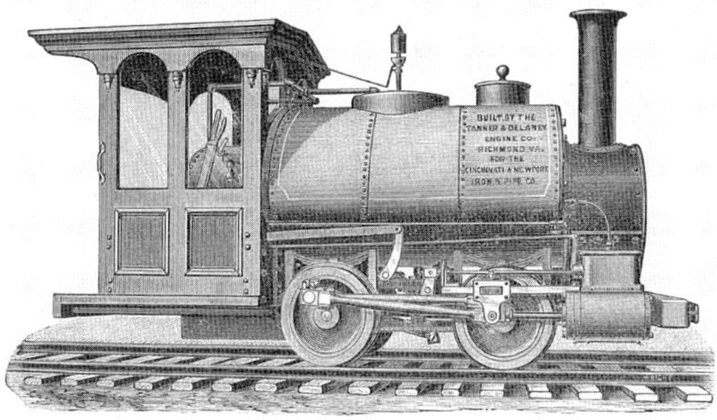

Top: Advertisement, Tanner & Delaney Narrow Gauge Locomotive *Governor Vance*, 1886. *John H. White Jr. Railroad Reference Collection, Archives Center, National Museum of American History, Smithsonian Institution.*

Bottom: Advertisement, Tanner & Delaney Narrow Gauge Locomotive, 1886. *John H. White Jr. Railroad Reference Collection, Archives Center, National Museum of American History, Smithsonian Institution.*

president, was deemed responsible for this failure and resigned in January 1887. Tanner left Richmond to found the Minnesota Iron Car Company in Duluth, Minnesota, where he stayed for four years before returning to Richmond. A tireless proponent of the cultivation of the musical arts throughout his life, serving as president of Richmond's Mozart Association as well as of the Richmond Musical and Benevolent Association, William E. Tanner died on August 6, 1898, after a prolonged illness, his tombstone declaring, "He has moved a little nearer to the master of all music."[126]

CHANGING OF THE GUARD

On January 5, 1887, in the offices of *Richmond Times* publisher Joseph Bryan, the Tanner & Delaney board of directors voted to appoint longtime investor William R. Trigg to succeed Tanner as president of the firm. Trigg had joined the company in 1884 as vice-president and treasurer and ascended to the presidency the very same day the board accepted Tanner's resignation.[127]

William R. Trigg. *From* Richmond Virginia: The City on the James, *1903.*

William Robertson Trigg was born on May 11, 1849, in Richmond and was named after his uncle, former Virginia delegate and acting Virginia governor (1836–37) Wyndham Robertson.[128] Educated in Richmond, he spent many summers at a relative's home in Fluvanna County; during one such excursion, an adolescent Trigg was briefly captured by patrolling Union soldiers, an anecdote he retained all his life as his one direct encounter with the North over the course of the Civil War. Trigg's railroad experience began early, with his employment as station agent at the age of 14 for the Richmond & Danville Railroad shortly before war's end.[129] Following a brief stint in Richmond banking, Trigg served as treasurer for the Richmond & West Point Terminal Railway and Warehouse Company, before joining Tanner & Delaney in 1884.[130] Prior to assuming presidency of the firm, Trigg was already a voluble proponent of further industrialism in Richmond and ran in the same circles as many of Richmond's most prominent men, including Joseph Bryan, Tredegar's Joseph R. Anderson, and tobacco magnate Lewis Ginter. Indeed, Trigg was present at the founding of Richmond's prestigious Commonwealth Club, alongside Anderson and Bryan, as well as James H. Dooley, Charles E. Bolling, and Peter H. Mayo, and was elected president of the club at, or shortly after, the organization's inception.[131]

Alexander Delaney's resignation would follow shortly after Tanner's, although not in as ignominious a manner, in May 1887. A grand celebration in his honor was held at the plant and attended by many of his workers, a majority of whom had served under Delaney since the firm's earliest years; he was presented with a gold watch and chain by the workmen, and Delaney's virtues, tireless dedication to work, and high esteem in the eyes of both his peers and subordinates were extolled by a series of speakers, including Chief Engineer William Simpkin and President Trigg. Toasts were made, to both Delaney and to a long and prosperous future for the Tanner & Delaney Engine Company. "Mr. Delaney replied in a few telling remarks, thanking those present for their kindness and assuring them that they would ever hold a place in his heart."[132] Delaney, along with his wife, Eliza Ahern, whom he had wed in 1868, relocated south to Petersburg briefly, where he became a partner in the works of Tappey & Delaney. The firm, whose senior partner was William H. Tappey, a native of Germany who had worked for some time in Richmond foundries before the Civil War, manufactured "Stationary, Portable & Hoisting Engines, Tram Road Engines and Car Irons, Hydraulic Pumps and Presses, and Tobacco Machinery," and other items, according to the company's circulars.[133] Delaney had returned to Richmond by 1892 and was a partner in the Richmond Iron Works, the history of which will be explored in subsequent pages. On March 1, 1895, Delaney was appointed engineer of the city's pump houses, during a meeting recorded by newspapers as "one of the most stormy on record," with Delaney having been elected only on the 21st ballot, despite the presence of former business partner Colonel Tanner on the Water Committee.[134] Delaney, in his new capacity, was charged with maintaining the level of water in, and the proper workings of the machinery servicing, Richmond's reservoirs; he also oversaw the installation of the municipality's first electric-powered water pumps and designed marked improvements on the valve seats at the city Pump House, today the Byrd Park Pump House.[135] At his home on Grove Avenue, Alexander Delaney died on March 23, 1910, at the age of 80; the *Times Dispatch* featured a lengthy obituary celebrating his life, a man the newspaper proclaimed "had one of the most unique and interesting careers of any citizen of Richmond."[136]

The Delaney legacy, however, continued on for some time. Chester Alexander Delaney, son of family patriarch Matthew, had joined his cousin at their namesake firm by the 1880s. After Alexander's resignation, Chester remained, eventually becoming assistant superintendent and later chief superintendent, a period during which he patented at least one invention, an improvement on lubricators for connecting rods, in 1894.[137] In 1898, Chester moved to Pennsylvania, following his appointment to the position of superintendent of the Dickson Locomotive Works, in Scranton.

3

THE RICHMOND LOCOMOTIVE AND MACHINE WORKS

1887–1901

On November 9, 1887, a meeting of the Tanner & Delaney Engine Company's board of directors was convened in order to chart a new course—that of entry into mainline locomotive manufacturing, a move signified by a vote to alter the name of the company to the Richmond Locomotive and Machine Works, with William Trigg as president, J.J. Montague as vice-president, George F. Jones as secretary, and R.D. Hudgins as treasurer.[138] At times, the "Machine" portion of the name was dropped, and it was referred to simply as the Richmond Locomotive Works. Much like Trigg's appointment to president following Tanner's ousting, Montague may have been chosen as vice-president based on his demonstrated business and financial acumen, in hopes of placing the Works on more stable footing. Montague was a well-respected Richmond businessman, having made his name in the lumber and manufacturing trades; his Montague Manufacturing Company, at the intersection of Arch and 9th Streets just north of the James River, produced items such as doors, sashes, balusters, mouldings, and blinds, while his lumber trade carried everything from pine to poplar.[139] Montague's association with the company far predates his appointment as vice-president, as he had joined Tanner, Ehbets, and Delaney at the founding of the Metropolitan Iron Works in 1865 as manager of the firm's sash, blinds, and door business, the assets of which he purchased outright three years later to carry on in his own name.[140]

While preparing to enter the mainline market, both before and following its reorganization as the Richmond Locomotive and Machine Works, the

J.J. Montague. *From* Richmond Virginia: The City on the James, *1903.*

firm continued to seek and fulfill municipal and private contracts that had served it well in years past, such as for two 25-horsepower hoisting engines in late 1887 for use in constructing Richmond's new City Hall along Broad Street.[141] The following year, the Richmond Union Passenger Railway, the world's first electric trolley system, purchased 20 streetcars from the Works, to the exacting designs of system engineer Frank J. Sprague.[142]

Much like Joseph R. Anderson at Tredegar some 40 years prior, Trigg also perceived the possible windfalls to be gained in federal contracts, specifically for the manufacture of steamship engines for the U.S. Navy. To that end, Trigg and William Simpkin, who had succeeded Alexander Delaney as superintendent, undertook several travels to Washington, D.C., to convince government officials and bureaucrats as to the worth of their Works, Trigg often entertaining a number of senators and congressmen at his home at 417 West Franklin Street, in an effort to secure their favors.[143] Inspectors from the U.S. Navy visited the Works in February 1888, to determine its suitability to construct engines for the pre-dreadnaught battleship USS *Texas*, a contract Trigg was emphatically seeking at the time; his efforts and courting of officials paid off, as the Works was selected from among six other bidders and awarded the *Texas*'s $634,000 contract on May 30, 1889. Any enthusiasm Trigg may have experienced from this victory was fleeting, however, as one hindrance after another seemed to plague the project. A terrible fire swept through the facility the night of January 14, 1891, destroying the boiler shop specifically dedicated to the *Texas* project. The fire was so intense that there was not enough water on hand to extinguish the blaze; nearby Shockoe Creek was temporarily dammed to divert additional water to the Works.[144] While Trigg was quick to assuage any concerns that work on the *Texas* would be adversely affected, the loss of the boiler shop proved detrimental enough that the government extended the completion time by a further eight months, to July 30, 1893. By the time the engines were ready to be installed, the government had failed to complete the vessel's hull at the Norfolk Navy Yards, so an indock trial of the engines was carried out; the engines performed well, perhaps too well, as a nearby schooner, the *H.W. Slicer*, was drawn into the *Texas*'s propellers and destroyed, resulting in $600 worth of damages, at the Works' expense.[145]

Mainline Engine Construction

With Trigg now at the helm and at least one lucrative government contract under his belt, shareholders' hopes for not only stability but further growth were bolstered with the new president's emphatic insistence on aggressive expansion into mainline locomotive construction, more than $200,000 worth of tools and equipment purchased in 1888, solely for locomotive fabrication.[146]

The year 1887's locomotive output consisted largely of engines for use along small railroads and company lines, such as the 0-4-0 ordered on behalf of the Sheffield Steel Company for use on its railroad, and a second of the same type for the Sloss Iron & Steel Company the following year, both of Alabama. Major lines do not appear in the Works order list until the following year, with a 2-6-0 sent to the RF&P, the first of many that the Works would produce for that line. The number of locomotives produced annually rose slowly, but steadily. The full first year of specialized locomotive production, 1887, saw 11 engines shipped out, the largest a 2-6-0 purchased on behalf of G.W. Wright & Co.; 1888 saw an increase of only 1 over the previous year; 1889–90 inclusive yielded 43 finished locomotives; 1891, 23; 1892, 65; and 1893, 82. The Richmond & Danville Railroad was the firm's largest purchaser in its first few years of mainline production, receiving 15 locomotives in total in 1889–90. Within a few years, as the company's reputation for quality grew, railroads began placing more substantial orders. In 1892, the single largest recipient of Richmond engines was the C&O, with 46 locomotives; in 1893, it was the Cleveland, Cincinnati, Chicago & St. Louis Railway, with 60.[147] The company recorded total sales of $344,884.35 in 1887; by 1890, that had risen to $710,350.53 and $940,204.53 in 1893.[148]

The process by which mainline locomotives were constructed in Richmond would have differed largely from most work performed previously by the company, although the fabrication of the pole road and other narrow-gauge locomotives would have been similar, albeit on a smaller scale. Unfortunately, nothing remains regarding the internal, day-to-day operations at the Richmond Locomotive Works; however, owing to knowledge of the facility's

Richmond Locomotive and Machine Works, circa 1891. *Cook Collection, Valentine Museum.*

layout as well as the detailed descriptions of operations at comparable works of the day, a process can be gleaned.

By the 1850s, railroads did not order from a catalogue of mass-produced locomotives but rather submitted detailed requests for highly customized items, everything from boiler specifications to cylinder size to valve gear requirements—all components could be manufactured according to the customer's specialized request.[149] This "made-to-order" method had its origins in the workshops of the earliest locomotive producers, innovators in a newborn field fashioning what was, in their minds, the engines best suited to whatever job or order was at hand. This mindset evolved into locomotive manufacturers constructing engines attuned to the exacting preferences of each railroad's chief engineer, master mechanics in their own right. With engines largely standardized only so far as function, many locomotives were unique unto themselves, in one way or another. In addition to cementing (ideally) a loyal customer base, satisfied that their exact needs would be recognized and respected in future orders, such a production model also allowed builders to keep abreast of the latest technological developments, as railroads were often eager to experiment with promising new designs and innovations. The highly customizable nature of locomotive production, and its successful utilization, was perfected by the Baldwin Locomotive Works of Philadelphia, the largest locomotive producer for most of the late nineteenth and early twentieth centuries. Like many producers of the time desiring similar success and seeking competitiveness, the Richmond

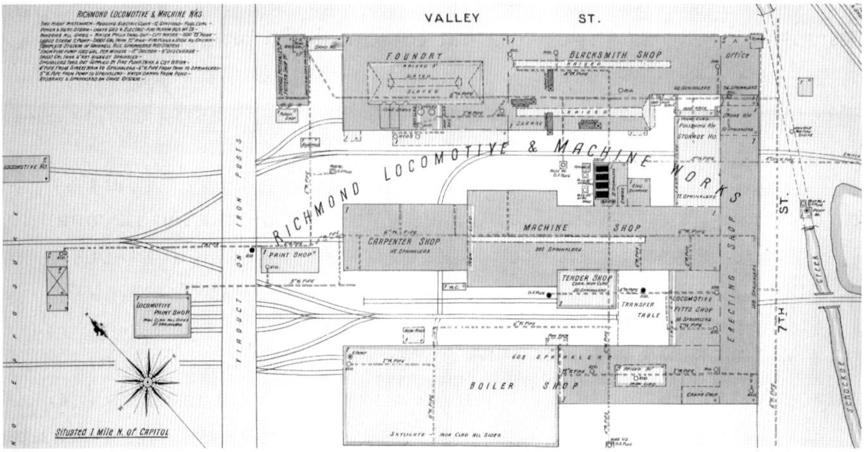

Richmond Locomotive and Machine Works, 1895. Sanborn Insurance Maps. *Library of Congress, Geography and Map Division, Sanborn Maps Collection.*

Locomotive Works would have emulated such practices as much as its means and manpower allowed. On the other hand, this symbiotic relationship, what has often been called a "feast-or-famine" business model, could prove far more detrimental than that experienced by other capital goods producers. During prosperous times, locomotive shops could rely on steady orders and a dedicated workforce. In the event of a recession, locomotive producers could very easily find themselves with orders slowing to a trickle, if arriving at all; the possibility of heavy losses due to a now-defunct railroad having ordered locomotives already under construction on credit; and the temporary shutdown of production entirely until orders recommenced, throwing thousands of men out of work for weeks or months.

Although each locomotive was produced according to a purchaser's individual demands, the actual practice of constructing a locomotive would have been largely homogenous, industry-wide, over the course of the last half of the nineteenth century.[150] What follows is a severely truncated account of the massive amount of toil, undertaken in sweltering environs and under the deafening and unrelenting clamor of the shop floors, required to produce a locomotive engine. Once a customer's order was finalized and processed, including all special requests and customizations noted, each department was given precise instructions as to the details for the part, or parts, entrusted to their care, with meticulous drawings provided by the firm's draftsmen. Foundrymen, using sand moulds, would cast valve boxes and cylinders—components, owing to their unique designs and internal structures, that could only be produced via casting. The Works' carpenter shop (and later an enlarged pattern shop) would have been responsible for creating the moulds used in the casting of such items, as well as accoutrements made of wood, such as seat boxes and foot boards.[151] Cast-iron wheels would have been produced in the foundry as well, although surviving Tredegar records show that the Locomotive Works often purchased wheels from that establishment, in frequently large quantities. For heavier items, and those that were to suffer the most stresses along the rails—such as connecting rods and axles—stronger wrought iron was needed and produced via the use of enormous steam hammers; this durability was also required for the locomotive frame itself and boiler. By the early 1870s, as the adoption and widespread use of the Bessemer process made steel much more affordable, many of the wrought-iron components of the locomotive had been replaced by those of steel. By the time the Works entered the mainline market, nearly all of the formerly wrought-iron parts were increasingly being substituted with steel.[152]

Any parts requiring further refinement were dispatched to the machine shops for finishing. Boilers were produced, appropriately enough, in the boiler shop, the boilermakers among the most skilled and respected men at any locomotives works. The casings for boilers were made from strips of wrought iron heated and rolled into plate and then rivetted together to enclose the boiler tubes. Multiple workers would work on a single boiler throughout its creation; when riveting the plates together, one worker on the outside of the cylindrical boiler casing hammered the red-hot rivets, which had been passed from a second worker to a third, stationed within the casing, who placed them into their respective apertures and applied opposite pressure against the hammer's strikes.[153] A combination of inconsistent quality of the iron rolled into boiler plate, as well as potential weaknesses at the seams, was the source of many boiler explosions in the early years of locomotive manufacture. As stated, by the time Trigg was aggressively seeking mainline orders, practices had advanced, and steel was being utilized at an increasing level.[154] Once all of the component pieces were ready, work moved to the erecting shop, in earlier years via manual labor and pullies, and later with large, overhead cranes. In the erecting shop, the boiler was leveled and joined to the frame and wheels; cylinders and boiler tubes were installed, followed by every other requisite component as the engine neared completion. Among the last to be installed were the valve gear, the coupling rods, the eccentrics—everything that actually made the locomotive, motive. Following completion and inspection, the engine was tested, "giving her

Left: Advertisement, Richmond Locomotive and Machine Works, circa 1889. *Nathan Vernon Madison.*

Below: Locomotive Construction, Erecting Shop, circa 1910, location unknown. *Nathan Vernon Madison.*

a good blowing out," to expel any dirt or other contaminants that could hinder the engine's functionality.[155] After paint and any other last-minute embellishments were applied, the engine was ready for shipment. Attention to an individual engine did not wholly cease upon its construction and shipment, as most locomotive shops carried supplies of spare parts that could be shipped along with the engine, as well as ordered at any time throughout the life of the locomotive. Railroad repair shops could then replace needed parts or retool these spare parts if need be, to better align with the chief engineers' understanding of what would best serve their line's needs.[156]

Organized Labor and the Richmond Locomotive Works

Throughout much of the country before the Civil War, and particularly in the less industrialized South, most products were manufactured in the home, with the conditions needed to create a widespread market for consumer goods not truly arriving until the advent of canals and later railroads. As these networks grew and more goods previously produced in the home were available for purchase, labor was increasingly unfettered for use in the industrial sector, in something of a self-replicating cycle.[157] While this was not an overnight transition even in the North, it was far slower below the Mason-Dixon line; as late as 1870, barely more than 10 percent of the southern states' populations lived in the region's urban centers, where, certainly in the case of Richmond, much of the area's industrial endeavors were likely to materialize.[158] High levels of immigration due to agricultural, economic, and political disasters in Europe aided in the growth of many of America's major cities, where industry and retail work offered ready employment to those newly arrived, bolstering the development of an emerging working class. In Richmond, the number of immigrants arriving in the city declined after the war; however, those who had come before, their children, and the large number of freedmen ensured a strong base from which industry could draw workers, skilled or otherwise, alongside those already present in the city in need of work. It was not until after the Civil War that organized unions began to exert a sizable influence over Richmond industry.

Founded in 1869, the Noble and Holy Order of the Knights of Labor grew from a small number of Philadelphia garment workers operating a secret society heavily inspired by the Freemasons to a union of national prominence. The Knights reached peak membership in 1886 at approximately 750,000, and unlike the many craft unions that were open solely to those of a particular trade, the Knights offered membership to workers from all professions. Local assemblies could be composed of either "trade assemblies," those composed of workers largely from a single profession or of workers who did not share a single trade, in what were known as "mixed assemblies."[159] The Knights first made their presence known in Richmond with the formation of Local Assembly No. 3157 in the spring of 1884, and within the next seven months the total number of assemblies in Richmond totaled six, largely under the direction of local printer and staunch labor reformer William H. Mullen. Soon, well over 10,000 workers belonged to assemblies across the city.[160]

The Knights spread their influence across the multitude of trades existing in Richmond at the time—from coopers at tobacco warehouses and machinists in iron and machine shops, to hewers of granite and those in the typographical trades, and scores of others. A significant number of these members, well over 3,000, were African American, as the Knights argued for a brotherhood devoid of racial animosity, a fact that was welcomed by reformers and African Americans recognizing the voice they now held as free members of a developing working class.[161] The Knights held their annual convention, or General Assembly, in Richmond in October 1886, a period now recognized as the organization's zenith. Due to both resistance (particularly in the South) to the Knights' promotion of racial equality and increased anti-union activities on the part of employers in the face of mounting labor strikes—443 in 1884, 645 in 1885, and 1,432 in 1886—the Knights began to lose adherents nationally, and the organization slowly ebbed away into obscurity.[162] Craft unions continued to exist and exert considerable force in Richmond industry following the collapse of the Knights, as demonstrated by labor issues that arose from time to time at the Richmond Locomotive Works.

As the Richmond Locomotive Works was home to the largest single concentration of mechanics and machinists in the city, union membership was naturally going to be high, both individual craft unions and, at the peak of its prominence, assemblies of the Knights of Labor. From all appearances, William E. Tanner and Alexander Delaney were respected by their workmen and did not display the tendency to suspect their workers as ready to "turn traitor" at any moment, as many industrialists of the day certainly did. In late January 1886, when workers demanded higher wages, Tanner and Delaney reached an amicable agreement to increase the pay of all machinists in their employ by 10 percent.[163] Likewise, there seemed

Employees inside the Richmond Locomotive and Machine Works Erecting Shop, circa 1891. *Cook Collection, Valentine Museum.*

to be no animosity between management and the Knights of Labor, whose executive board the company had joined in negotiations with to secure that 10 percent raise; following the Knights' General Assembly that same year, all the "tables, benches, wood-work, and drapery" used at the gathering were donated for use in a bazaar held to benefit the Little Sisters of the Poor at Richmond's Armory Hall, an event overseen by Alexander Delaney's wife, Eliza.[164] At Delaney's farewell dinner in 1887, among the chosen speakers, alongside President Trigg and Chief Engineer Simpkin, was Joseph Devine, a prominent and outspoken Knight of Labor and Reform Republican in Richmond politics. A boilermaker by trade, Devine was well respected in labor circles and was an ardent ally of William H. Mullen, now Knight of Labor Executive Board member and publisher of the city's Knights organ, the *Labor Herald*.[165] During his speech, Devine provided accounts of Delaney's virtues, as well as testimonials from the workmen, attesting to the "esteem and regard in which he was held by the employes who had been so long connected with him."[166]

With Delaney's departure, the workingmen had seemingly lost a sympathetic ear to their plights, as Trigg evidently did not hold labor unions in high regard. He, alongside directors such as Joseph Bryan, believed unions to be an irritant in the promulgation of the hierarchal, paternalistic society they envisioned for Richmond and the larger South. Trigg, Bryan, and many of their societal peers showed greater favor to institutions such as the Virginia Mechanics Institute or even unions run by the company itself—anything that would deter workers from seeing themselves as a class, in and among themselves, thus preventing their fall into the "radicalization" that, in their minds, was a hallmark of worker-led unions.[167]

On March 19, 1891, 150 machinists, many of whom were working on the battleship *Texas* boilers, called a strike in response to what they considered an overreach on the part of management. They were of a generation cognizant of the power they held as an organized, working class, while also rooted in the traditions of a guild system, wherein apprentices learned from masters over the course of several years to become master tradesmen themselves. The machinists (who made between $2.50 and $3.00 a day) objected when an unskilled man (paid between $1.25 and $1.75) was put to work on an axle-lathe, a machine they felt should be handled only by one of their own. When management rejected the formation of a committee to address the issue, the workmen walked out in protest.[168] The union at the heart of the strike, the International Association of Machinists (IAM, today's International Association of Machinists and Aerospace Workers), which had its national headquarters in Richmond at the time, covered the walkout extensively in its monthly journal, calling it "what will be known in Richmond as the greatest effort the mechanics have ever made in this city." "Not only did union men go out," the IAM argued, "but the non-union men also. It was not a question of unionism, but one in which the principle of every mechanic was involved, and they responded to the call upon their manhood like true American citizens, and resolved to nip the bud before it blossomed."[169] What both management and fellow workers expected to be resolved the next day was only perpetuated three days later, when all moulders, soon joined by the Works' carpenters and blacksmiths, went on strike as well. The company came to a near standstill as a working population of around 500 men across several departments dwindled to 25 or so.

E.F.C. Davis, formerly of the Philadelphia & Reading Coal & Iron Co. and member of the American Society of Mechanical Engineers, was the Works' general manager at the time. Davis was an ardent opponent of unionization, having boasted "since assuming control of the works that he would not

Employees outside the Richmond Locomotive and Machine Works, northern side of the complex with the 5th Street Viaduct visible, circa 1891. *Cook Collection, Valentine Museum.*

recognize trades unions of any kind, and that he had broken the backbone of the Machinists' Union in Richmond and that he would do the same with the moulders." It was actually Davis's reply to the moulders (those primarily tasked with working with sand moulds and castings in the foundry), when they expressed concern for the plight of their fellow workmen, that "they were barking up the wrong tree," that led them to follow the machinists in walking out.[170] As the strike went on, odds seemed to be in the workmen's favor, with each group's respective unions supplying relief funds, and many of the strikers were even offered positions at the Newport News Dry-Dock and Steamship Company, if no resolution with Davis was forthcoming.

And forthcoming a resolution was not. Despite claims on the part of management and President Trigg himself that the "company wins the victory" with nearly 400 men engaged at the Works (composed nearly entirely of new workers), picketers still patrolled outside all entrances to the plant, cautioning all who approached not to seek employment with such an establishment.[171] On June 4, 1891, machinists at the city's C&O shops sent an open letter to T.S. Lloyd, master mechanic of the railroad's shops, requesting the company, in solidarity with the strikers, halt the usage and purchasing of castings produced by the Works for the remainder of the strike's duration. The C&O workers maintained that "while we do not wish to place ourselves in the attitude of dictating to our employers where they shall have their work done we consider that as union men and members of the International Association of Machinists we are not doing that justice to our fellow-men which we think is justly due them" by continuing to use products purchased from a company that so blatantly ignored the "apprenticeship system."[172] T.S. Lloyd, to his credit, replied in a much more conciliatory tone to his workmen than Davis did his own, stating that the contract with the Works was signed long before the "current troubles" began, and it would be a breach of contract and outside of good faith to simply cancel the order now. However, Lloyd also suggested that if any workers, after taking his explanation into account, felt they could not conduct themselves in service to the C&O, their resignations would certainly be accepted.

As the strike persisted, the Richmond Locomotive Works augmented its workforce with new recruits. A recently installed 60,000-pound steam hammer was in full use, and as of August 1891, approximately 30 locomotives were in various stages of construction, as were the materials for the battleship *Texas*, work on which had floundered briefly as a result of the strike.[173] The IAM claimed that the work produced in those months was nothing short of shoddy and that the "scabs" producing these engines were merely adding unskilled finishing touches to machines already largely completed before the strike began. Additionally, it was claimed that management was not only sending agents to Pennsylvania and other states to secure replacement workers, but also pressuring other establishments in Richmond to reject any strikers seeking employment elsewhere.[174] Much to the dismay of the union, the succeeding months saw many of the strikers returning to work and the movement fizzling out; by February of the following year, the workforce was nearly fully restored (by either returning workers or new hires), and regular business recommenced. The aforementioned dip in locomotives shipped in 1891 and 1892 (23 and 65, respectively) is likely a result of work delays brought by the strike. In March 1893, Richmond sent a 2-8-0 locomotive (also known as a Consolidation type, named after the first engine to have used such a wheel configuration) to Chicago for display at the World's Fair. With the most modern of Westinghouse automatic air brakes and other state-of-the art components, the engine and accompanying tender, nearly 200,000 pounds collectively

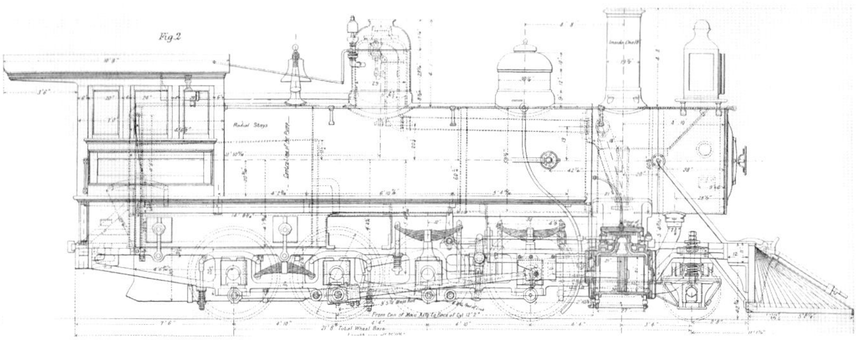

Top: Chesapeake & Ohio No. 350, 1893, 2-8-0. Built for exhibition at the 1893 Chicago World's Fair. *Nathan Vernon Madison.*

Bottom: Chesapeake & Ohio No. 350, 1893, 2-8-0. Built for exhibition at the 1893 Chicago World's Fair. *Nathan Vernon Madison.*

when in use, were based on the designs of C&O superintendent of motive power William Garstang. Order No. 2337 (No. 350 in the C&O system) was a success at the fair and a public repudiation that the "troubles" of 1891 represented any long-term impediments for the company.[175]

Work on the *Texas* neared completion, and this project came to be a source of pride for both the workmen involved and for the city itself. During a parade to celebrate the Democratic victories in the November 1892 elections, which saw Grover Cleveland elected for his second (nonconsecutive) term as president, over 700 locomotive workmen marched through the city. President Trigg and Joseph Bryan preceded the men and their float—a full-scale facsimile of one of the four 123,000-pound boilers intended for the vessel.[176] Labor concerns, for the moment, certainly seemed to be in the past: following the parade, a sumptuous lunch was held on the grounds

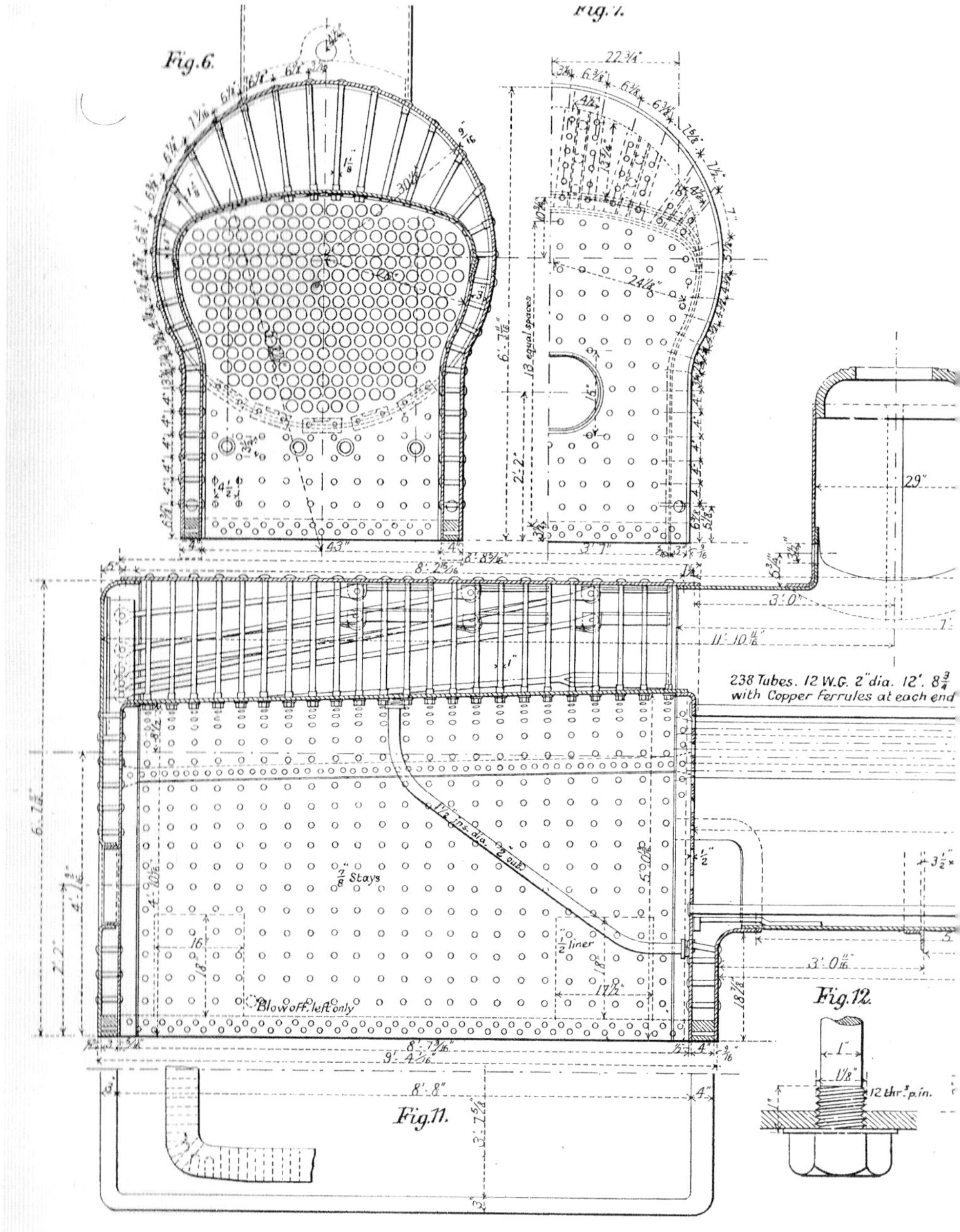

Boiler and other components, Chesapeake & Ohio No. 350, 1893, 2-8-0. Built for exhibition at the 1893 Chicago World's Fair. *Nathan Vernon Madison.*

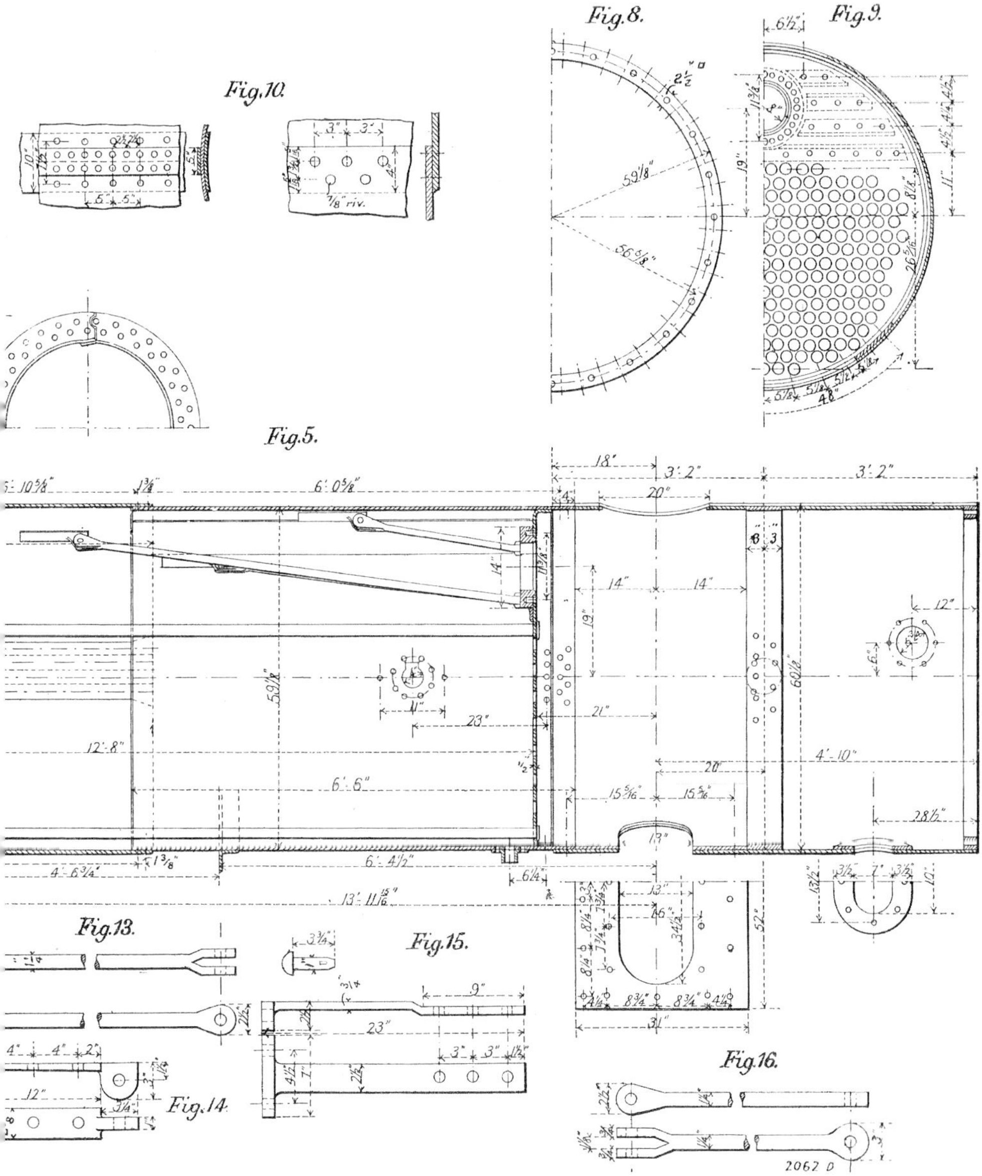
Fig.10.
Fig.8.
Fig.9.
Fig.5.
Fig.13.
Fig.15.
Fig.14.
Fig.16.
2062 D

of the Richmond Howitzer's armory, presented on the part of Trigg and associates, to their workers. After the meal, "a vote of thanks…was tendered the officers and directors of the Locomotive Works for the kindness and care for their employees displayed on this and all other occasions."[177]

Setbacks, Innovations and Challenges

With the onset of the Panic of 1893, Richmonders' pride in the Richmond Locomotive Works went hand in hand with their belief in its strength and durability as a going concern. The Panic of 1893 was influenced by a myriad of factors, the failure of the Philadelphia & Reading Railroad just one of many. The Reading, following a period of costly overexpansion that drew the ire and stock manipulations on the part of John Pierpont Morgan, collapsed into bankruptcy. The Reading, once among the largest companies on Earth, was a major carrier of Pennsylvania's anthracite coal, on which most of America was heavily reliant.[178] Not dissimilar to the "domino effect" that caused a panic two decades prior, Reading's collapse led to the failure of many financing firms and related companies that were dependent on the railroad. Instability in Europe and a poor crop throughout America's agricultural regions brought further burdens. Between 1890 and 1893, the amount of gold held in the U.S. Treasury dropped from $190 million to $100 million, due in some part to the passage of the Sherman Silver Purchase Act of 1890. America was on the gold standard, and the dwindling amount of the precious metal in federal repositories caused concerns regarding the convertibility of notes into gold, prompting runs on banks and federal depositories. By the end of the year, over 15,000 businesses of various sizes and 500 banks had collapsed in an economic catastrophe that did not truly begin to subside until 1897.[179] In 1895, at the height of the panic, J.P. Morgan and the influential Rothschild family sold 3.5 million ounces of gold at a cost of $65 million to the U.S. Treasury to prevent what many saw as an inevitable default on the part of the U.S. government.[180]

During such turbulent times, many clearinghouses and banks issued scrip, as did manufacturers to pay their workers, backed only by the holder's faith in the stability of the issuing institution. The Richmond Locomotive and Machine Works issued scrip in August 1893 in response to the scarcity of paper currency at the time, in $1, $2, $5, $10, and $20 denominations.[181] The Works was seen as dependable enough that many local businesses accepted the scrip just as readily as they would U.S. Treasury notes. "We not only take certified checks, but will take the [Richmond Locomotive and Machine Works] scrip at full face value payable in our goods," read an ad in the *Richmond Times*, on the part of grocers Vashon & Rose, at the corner of 6th Street and Clay. "We also take the same, giving orders on dry goods and other merchants, if desired. We will do all we can to accommodate the man in need."[182] Faith in the Works was maintained, even if business seemed to wane in the worst years of the panic. The shops closed briefly, and the company sold many of its boilers, cranes, and other machinery for relatively low prices. Orders placed in 1893 and early the following year dipped significantly, with 1894 showing only 27 shipped locomotives; however, in 1895 that total rose to 67, a sign that the worst of the panic was beginning to recede.

In August 1895, general manager E.F.C. Davis died following a horse-riding accident. Davis was succeeded by Carl Johan Mellin, who was originally hired five years prior as a machinist on the battleship *Texas* project.[183] Mellin was born on February 17, 1851, in Västergötland, Sweden, and served as an engineer in his homeland before immigrating to Scotland in the late 1880s to work at the Caledonian Locomotive Works in Glasgow and then to America, serving as mechanical engineer for New York's Dynamite Gun Company, from 1887 through 1889, at which point he relocated to Richmond.[184] Mellin demonstrated his expertise during his work on the *Texas* and, more

Chesapeake & Western No. 102, 1895, 4-4-0. *Nathan Vernon Madison.*

importantly, on previous naval projects in Scotland, where he came to be an authority on the construction of compound engines for steamships—expertise he would adapt to locomotive engines in Richmond. The so-called simple engines of most locomotives lost a great deal of potential energy in the form of exhaust steam that was not put to any practical use but rather simply expelled from the engine. In an attempt to increase the efficiency of locomotives, in terms of both steam produced and water spent doing so, without increasing the weight or size of the engine, compound engines were designed to essentially recycle this spent steam and generate supplementary power by forcing it from the initial high-pressure cylinders into secondary low-pressure cylinders, the number of cylinders in each stage differing from model to model. The cross compound, or a compound engine with two cylinders (one high pressure, one low pressure), that Mellin specialized in, and the simplest of the several compound varieties, soon became one of the Works' signature products. The C&O purchased the first of Mellin's compounds in 1892, the 4-6-0 No. 140, which recorded more than a 20 percent increase in efficiency over other compounds.[185]

Another of Mellin's 4-6-0 compounds, an engine designated No. 2427 in company rolls, was built as a kind of spokesman for the line and for the Richmond Locomotive and Machine Works itself. Completed in 1894, No. 2427 spent the next several years traveling across the United States and Europe. The *Richmond Tramp*, as No. 2427 affectionately came to be called on account of its globetrotting, was part of the company's exhibit at the Exposition Universelle, or Paris Exposition, of 1900, a world's fair that recorded nearly 50 million attendees over several months; following its world tour, the *Tramp* was sold to California's Randsburg Railway.[186] While simple engines still accounted for the majority of Richmond's outcome in terms of locomotive engines, more than 150 compounds of Mellin's design were constructed at Richmond in the years between 1895 and 1901. Many companies also purchased machinery from the Works that allowed for upgrading their simple engines into compounds along Mellin's pattern.[187]

Despite the recognition the Richmond Locomotive Works had enjoyed since its reorganization, there was a natural suspicion on the part of many northern manufacturers and investors about the quality, or lack thereof, of southern industry, a sentiment that had been entrenched for decades. Touring the Works in 1890 during a visit by the Master Mechanics Association, editor of *Locomotive Engineer* and venerated expert on all things related to the railroading industry Angus Sinclair said of the Richmond plant: "The sum of the opinions expressed was that these were remarkably

Richmond Locomotive and Machine Works No. 2427, *The Richmond Tramp*. Built for Exhibition, 1894, 4-6-0. *John H. White Jr. Railroad Reference Collection, Archives Center, National Museum of American History, Smithsonian Institution.*

good shops *for the south*, and that the work turned out was highly creditable *for a southern shop*."[188] Sinclair noted not only what he deemed deficiencies in the facility itself but also in the standards of the workmen. "Very free and easy practices prevail among the personnel of the works, men in responsible positions carrying convivial practices inside the gates, while the same people felt at liberty to go outside to enjoy liquid refreshments during work hours," Sinclair wrote of the Richmond shops in his seminal work, *Development of the Locomotive Engine* (1907).[189] Trigg and the firm's leadership recognized that new management on the Works' floor was needed, and in July 1897, they turned that responsibility over to H.A. Gillis, former general foreman and later master mechanic at the Roanoke Machine Works. Now general superintendent at Richmond, he faced the twofold undertaking of imposing some level of discipline on what some considered a lackadaisical approach to work on the part of its employees, as well as bringing the shops' level of efficacy more in line with that of their northern competitors, a task that Sinclair had compared to Hercules' legendary task of "clean[ing] the Augean stable."[190] Sinclair's opinion of the Works' efficacy was not unwarranted, as he noted that the firm relied too heavily on manual labor, usually on the part of the company's African American workforce, to conduct much work that could have been achieved far more efficiently through the use of modern "labor saving appliances." Not only was more professional conduct enforced among the workers thanks to Gillis's efforts, but the plant's operations were modernized as well. In place of a time- and labor-wasting practice of all work on the shop floors ceasing while a multitude of laborers carried machinery from one stage of construction to another, newly installed cranes were used to perform the same work, quickly and efficiently.[191] In later years, Joseph Bryan wrote to Gillis, concerning his influence on the Works' increased productivity:

> *How much of this striking and acknowledged improvement was due to your own wisdom and energy I cannot fully express herein. I will say, however, that I do not know another man who, better than you, could have filled the place which fell to your lot. The work which you and your associates did made possible an achieved success which was obstructed by difficulties apparently unsurmountable.*[192]

The year 1898 saw yet another significant change in the Work's management, when William R. Trigg resigned as president, although he still maintained a seat on the company's board of directors. Trigg left to establish a new concern: the William R. Trigg Shipbuilding Company. This new plant encompassed 45 acres and 12 buildings, occupying both sides of the remnants of the James River and Kanawha Canal on, and across from, Chapel Island.[193] Trigg's venture seemed promising at first and was celebrated as the birth of a new industry in Richmond, with naval contracts in December 1898 totaling over $900,000, including the construction of the navy destroyers *Dale* and *Decatur* at $260,000 each.[194] For the launching of the torpedo ship *Shubrick* in late October 1899, President William McKinley was in attendance and lauded both the ship and its builders, as well as "this great city upon its industrial revival and upon the notable prosperity it is feeling in all of its business enterprises."[195] The Trigg Yards, alongside the Richmond Locomotive and Machine Works and Tredegar, were heralded in papers and by city boosters as among the most important enterprises in Richmond.

It, therefore, undoubtedly came as a surprise to many when Trigg's enterprise, on December 23, 1902, suddenly entered receivership, with Trigg's nephew and company vice-president (now acting president, as well) Lilburn T. Myers serving as receiver. It soon came to light that the company had underbid to unrealistic levels on many of its contracts, errors compounded by its shortsightedness in not factoring in the likelihood of unforeseen design changes or cost overruns after construction had begun, resulting in enormous losses on nearly every ship it produced. In addition to

Left: H.A. Gillis, date unknown. *Library of Congress.*

Right: Construction of the USS *Dale* and USS *Decatur*, June 29, 1901, at the Trigg Shipyards. *NH 98173 Courtesy of the Naval History & Heritage Command.*

hemorrhaging capital, the Trigg company owed over $170,000 to various suppliers and held $1 million in outstanding mortgage bonds.[196] Myers took control of the receivership process, as Trigg was in no position to do so himself, having suffered a paralyzing stroke in January of the previous year, possibly brought on by the mounting stress of what he realized was an untenable business position.[197] Under receivership, the company continued to flounder. In January 1903, over $15,000 in wages owed to workmen was delayed by two weeks before finally being remitted.[198] On February 16, 1903, William Trigg, despite having been healthy enough to travel to Hot Springs, Arkansas, and other health resorts since his stroke, finally succumbed to his maladies, which by that point had grown to include an infection of the kidneys, and died at the age of 53.[199] His obituary's opinion that the William R. Trigg Shipbuilding Company's recent troubles seemingly "marks the shading of the first life of the plant into its second which all hope and believe will be abundantly useful and enduring" proved amaurotic to the true status of the enterprise.[200] Aside from labor on a tanker for the Standard Oil Company already initiated, work at the shipyards, which at one point had employed well over 1,000 men, largely ceased. After it was realized that there were not sufficient funds to pay the remaining workmen to whom wages were still owed ($20,000), Joseph Bryan offered $5,000 if other interests agreed to come up with the still-outstanding $15,000, with several city banks agreeing to supply the remainder.[201] After further lawsuits on the part of affected creditors, the plant closed. The property of the William R. Trigg Shipbuilding Company was put up for public auction on July 10, 1905, and sold to a pair of Philadelphia businessmen for the sum of $368,000, with various creditor grievances continuing for years to come.[202]

Joseph Bryan

The man most commonly associated today with the Richmond Locomotive Works, Joseph Bryan, was elected president of the company following William Trigg's resignation. Born on August 13, 1845, in Gloucester County, Joseph Bryan was the eighth child of plantation owner John Randolph Bryan and his wife, Elizabeth Tucker Coalter Bryan.[203] First educated by tutors at the family home of Eagle Point and later at the Episcopal High School in Alexandria, Bryan briefly served in the volunteer artillery regiment known as the Richmond Howitzers and later, as a member of Mosby's Raiders, during the Civil War. Bryan graduated from the University of Virginia in the summer of 1868 with a degree in law and established an office in Palmyra, Fluvanna County. Following his marriage to Isobel "Belle" Lamont Stewart in 1871 (in which William Trigg was counted among the groomsmen), Bryan settled at the Stewart family home of Brook Hill, just outside of Richmond, where he opened a law office the following year at 1002 Main Street in the city's downtown, just slightly downhill from the Capitol. Business was slow at first but began to improve with Bryan's involvement in several well-publicized cases, including a bond case involving the Richmond & Petersburg Railroad, followed by a suit brought by a dissatisfied investor in the Chesapeake and Ohio Canal that went first to the Washington, D.C. Supreme Court and then the United States Supreme Court in 1877.

In 1887, four years after purchasing the land on which he established his estate of Laburnum, Bryan entered into the business on which most of his legacy now rests, that of newspaper editor and publisher. The *Richmond Daily Times* (later shortened to *Richmond Times*) was founded by Major Lewis Ginter, with its first edition issued on October 22, 1886. Within a year's time, however, Ginter had lost interest in the paper, and its control soon passed into the hands of the Major's lawyer, Joseph Bryan. David Tennent Bryan recalled decades later, "Old Maj. Lewis Ginter wanted to unload The Richmond *Times* on my grandfather," free of charge, he was so tired of the whole affair.[204] Not only did Bryan keep the *Times* afloat, but he also made it a success and a true contender to the *Richmond Dispatch*, the city's

Joseph Bryan. *From* Richmond Virginia: The City on the James, *1903.*

other leading newspaper, founded in 1850. Bryan, harkening back to speeches and treatises he had produced years earlier against William Mahone's "Readjuster" movement, used the pages of the *Times* to vilify just as fervently the Free Silver platform championed by Williams Jennings Bryan in the 1890s, which resulted in a temporary, yet significant, drop in *Times* circulation, owing to the public popularity of the Free Silver argument. Under Bryan, the *Times* was a platform from which Conservative, Lost Cause narratives were argued for and defended. In 1903, Joseph Bryan and John Williams, who owned the *News* (founded 1899) as well as the *Dispatch*, agreed that the city had too many papers—the *Richmond Dispatch*, the *Times*, the *New*, and the *Evening Leader*, first issued in 1888 in Manchester—and that consolidation was the answer. It was then decided that Bryan would publish the merged *Richmond Times-Dispatch*, while Williams would be responsible for the combined *News Leader*. In 1908, Bryan purchased the *News Leader* from Williams, providing him with both a morning and evening paper, and with them a near monopoly over Richmond's newspapers.

Bryan was also heavily involved in the railroading and ironmaking industries, through which he believed a revitalization of the South could be had. Bryan, Trigg and many others, still holding to the sectionalism that had birthed the Confederacy, believed that a truly independent southern economy that could compete with, if not best, that of the North could be realized through fervent southern industrialization. He was a director of and significant stockholder in both the Richmond & Danville Railroad (R&D) and the Richmond & West Point Terminal Railroad and Warehouse Company, a holding company owned by the R&D and formed by Bryan with other R&D shareholders in 1880 to expand their influence over the region's railroads by acquiring controlling interests in noncontiguous lines—something the R&D's charter forbade but was acceptable on the part of a holding company.[205] In 1881, he became a director (and in 1889, president) of the Georgia Pacific Railway, and it was through these positions that Bryan became involved with several companies along the railroad's path, and in the process investing heavily in the growth of businesses and communities in and around Birmingham, Alabama. In 1887, Bryan and several of his Georgia Pacific partners took control of Birmingham's Sloss Iron and Steel Company; in 1899, Sloss was consolidated with several other regional iron works to form the Sloss-Sheffield Steel and Iron Company, which grew to become, by the time of the First World War, the world's chief producer of pig iron.[206]

Joseph Bryan first became associated with the Richmond Locomotive Works through mortgage bonds for the Tanner & Delaney Engine Company he purchased in the early 1880s, eventually becoming a significant voice in the company's management and, by 1887, accruing 30,000 shares, valued at $15,000.[207] Bryan maintained his belief in the promise of the locomotive and railroading industries, despite several financial setbacks in the 1890s, particularly the collapse of the R&D in 1892 and its ensuing receivership. Although Bryan's losses in the venture were significant and something he deemed a serious threat to his family's lifestyle, there was a silver lining in that the R&D's subsequent reorganization by J P. Morgan resulted in Bryan gaining a director's position in its successor, the Southern Railway Company.

Bryan, now president of the Richmond Locomotive Works, inherited several subordinates on whom he could rely to successfully oversee the various aspects of this new undertaking, a business in which he lacked much direct knowledge. Voting in favor of contracts or upgrades to the facilities was one thing; actively participating in the daily management of an enterprise as massive and complex as a locomotive factory was quite another. Chief among these valued subordinates was H.A. Gillis, who, in his role as general superintendent, did much to correct inefficient and backward practices, all the while offering suggestions for future improvements that could help elevate the Works to further national prominence.

Bryan could also depend on his closest assistant, Columbus K. Lassiter. Born in 1866, Lassiter first joined the industry as a blacksmith's apprentice at the age of 13, following the death of his father and the need to support the family. By the age of 20, after a few years working in a flour mill, he had opened his own bakery in Richmond. In 1892, he left that business for a $60 a month salary as timekeeper at the Richmond Locomotive Works, where he remained, eventually promoted to chief clerk to the president just as Bryan's tenure began.[208] Lassiter had demonstrated both business savvy as well as engineering prowess during his earliest days at the company. When informed that $0.15 was the cheapest that a particular bolt could be manufactured, Lassiter reconfigured the machinery in question so that, by the time he was done, the cost had been lessened to below a penny. Later, Lassiter informed management that the sales department had made a grievous error on a bid it submitted to produce locomotives for the Egyptian government by failing to include the cost of several vital components, including, surprisingly enough, the engines' wheels; thankfully, the bid was refused, averting the financial ruin of the company.[209] Recognizing Lassiter's mechanical and locomotive acumen, Trigg transferred the clerk from the office to the shop floor, a role in which Lassiter aided in the modernization and streamlining of many of the Works' operations. Lassiter was able to find innovative and cost-effective methods of procuring or manufacturing in-house essential components, such as establishing an additional foundry on-site to produce parts formerly purchased from outside vendors. Later in his career, he organized a hybrid salaried/piecework system that saw individual shops act as subcontractors on particular projects, an idea he brought to Richmond but one that had been in use at many factories for decades prior. "The pipe shop got a certain amount of money for their part of the job of piping locomotives," recalled Lassiter employee Thomas Green years later. "If the shop made $3,500 a week, the men who held the contract would deduct guaranteed salaries for all pipe-shop employees, keep 20 percent themselves, and divide the rest among the shopmen."[210] Lassiter also patented several inventions, including advancements in staybolt design, that provided "handsome royalties" for years to come.[211]

In later years, Bryan's son, John Stewart Bryan, wrote of his father's daily routine while president of the Richmond Locomotive Works. Working about the grounds of Laburnum in the early morning, Bryan would then bathe

EIGHT-WHEEL NARROW-GAUGE LOCOMOTIVE.

[Can also be Built for Standard Gauge.]

Cylinder Dia. and Stroke in Inches.	Driver Dia. in Inches.	Rigid Wheel Base.	Total Wheel Base.	Water Capacity of Tender Tank.	Weight in Working Order.	Hauling Capacity in Tons of 2,000 Pounds.
11x16	40	6.0	15.6	1,050 gallons.	35,500 pounds.	610
12x16	40 to 44	6.6	16.6	1,200 "	38,500 "	660
12x18	44 to 48	6.9	17.0	1,200 "	41,500 "	710
13x18	44 to 48	6 9	17.6	1,400 "	46,500 "	780

Advertisement, Richmond Locomotive and Machine Works, eight-wheel narrow-gauge locomotive, circa 1889. *John H. White Jr. Railroad Reference Collection, Archives Center, National Museum of American History, Smithsonian Institution.*

These Locomotives are particularly adapted for fast passenger service, and are capable of a speed of from 20 to 40 miles per hour. The wearing parts are well proportioned for this service, and the Boilers are very large.

Curves of 150 feet radius can be taken by these Engines. When the smaller size of drivers are used, these Locomotives are very efficient for mixed or for freight traffic.

SIX-WHEEL NARROW GAUGE LOCOMOTIVE, WITH TENDER.

[Can also be Built for Standard Gauge.]

Cylinder Dia and Stroke in Inches.	Driver Dia. in Inches.	Rigid Wheel Base.	Total Wheel Base.	Water Capacity of Tender Tank.	Weight in Working Order.	Hauling Capacity in Tons of 2,000 Pounds.
10x16	33 to 36	6 0	16.3	850 gallons.	32,500 pounds.	625
11x16	36 to 40	6.0	16.3	1,050 "	34,000 "	700
12x16	40 to 44	6.6	16.11	1,200 "	38,000 "	750
12x18	44 to 48	6.9	17.5	1,200 "	40,000 "	800
13x18	44 to 48	6.9	18.0	1,400 "	45,000 "	900

Advertisement, Richmond Locomotive and Machine Works, six-wheel narrow-gauge locomotive, with tender, circa 1889. *John H. White Jr. Railroad Reference Collection, Archives Center, National Museum of American History, Smithsonian Institution.*

and head to the office around noon, remaining there for as long as the day's business required, before retiring, not to his home, but to his desk at the *Times* to address the business of the paper before finally calling it a night. During the day, he would often have lunch at any number of restaurants downtown, either alone or among other Richmond business leaders. Oftentimes, he would take this midday meal in the company of his personal bookkeeper, one William Wortham Pool.[212] Students of Richmond's supernatural folklore will recognize Pool as the occupant of the tomb associated with the legend of the Richmond Vampire. Following a disastrous railroad tunnel collapse in the city's Church Hill district in 1925, several witnesses claimed to have observed a vampiric entity emerge from the rubble, run across the city to Hollywood Cemetery and enter Pool's mausoleum. This urban legend, however, has no bearing on a man understood by his contemporaries as an able businessman and pillar of his Manchester community; to quote *Richmond Magazine*'s Harry Kollatz Jr.: "While on occasion some accountants have been described as 'bloodsuckers,' whether such an actual definition can be applied to Pool remains a matter of idle conjecture."[213]

Under Bryan's stewardship, the Works' productivity continued to rise. In March 1899, while busily finishing work on 8 locomotives ordered by the Wabash Railroad, the company was nearing completion of a contract to manufacture 20 engines (10 heavy tanks and 10 freight engines, all 2-6-0s) for the Kingdom of Sweden. Under the supervision of a Swedish engineer, a trial run of the first engine of this order was made between Richmond and the port city of Norfolk, whence the engines were shipped across the Atlantic to Europe.[214] In December, perennial customer Seaboard ordered a further 25 ten-wheel freight 4-6-0s, as part of a massive expansion undertaken by the line that year.[215] In 1899, 116 completed locomotives left the Richmond Works and 186 in 1900; the Southern Railway, of which Joseph Bryan was a director, received a total of 46 Richmond locomotives (12 4-6-0s and 33 2-8-0s) in those two years alone. Between October 1898 and 1899, the costs of sending traveling salesmen across the country, singing the firm's praises and hopefully securing lucrative contracts, rose from $16,666 to $25,166; in October and November 1899 alone, the company spent over $91,000 on its exhibit at the National Export Exposition in Philadelphia.[216] Recorded sales had dipped in the wake of the Panic of 1893, with 1894 and 1895's numbers dropping to $597,112.61 and $554,374.44, respectively; by 1898, sales had rebounded to $920,009.55, and in 1899 they reached $1,303,065.90, nearly the equivalent of $47 million in 2022.[217] The Richmond Locomotive Works was consuming so much iron and steel that a group of Boston and Richmond businessmen proposed building a steel works in the city at the cost of around $2 million. Though floated about in newspapers and rumor mills for several months beginning in June 1900, touting such advantages as the amount of steel used throughout the city already and the proximity to the nearby Richmond Coal Basin, the plan, ultimately, never reached fruition.[218]

Early 1900 saw approximately 1,300 workers employed at the Works, running day and night on 12-hour shifts, with even the city doing its part

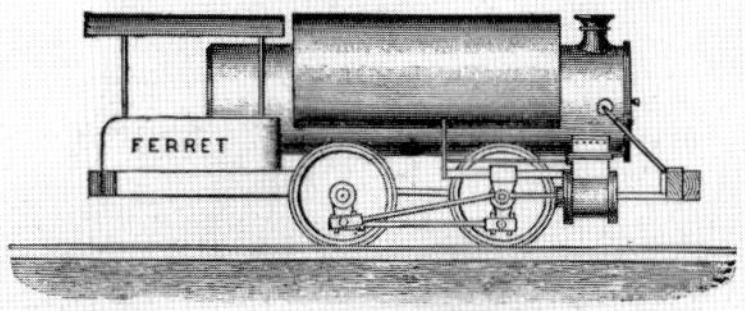

FOUR-WHEEL CONNECTED MINE LOCOMOTIVE.

Cylinder Diameter and Strokes in inches.	Driver Diameter in inches.	Wheel Base.	Water Capacity of Tank.	Weight in Working Order.	Hauling Capacity in Tons of 2,000 Pounds.
7x10	24	3.9	150 gallons.	12,000 pounds.	300
7x14	26	4.0	200 "	16,500 "	375
8x15	28	4.6	300 "	18,500 "	425

Advertisement, Richmond Locomotive and Machine Works, four-wheel connected mine locomotive, circa 1889. *John H. White Jr. Railroad Reference Collection, Archives Center, National Museum of American History, Smithsonian Institution.*

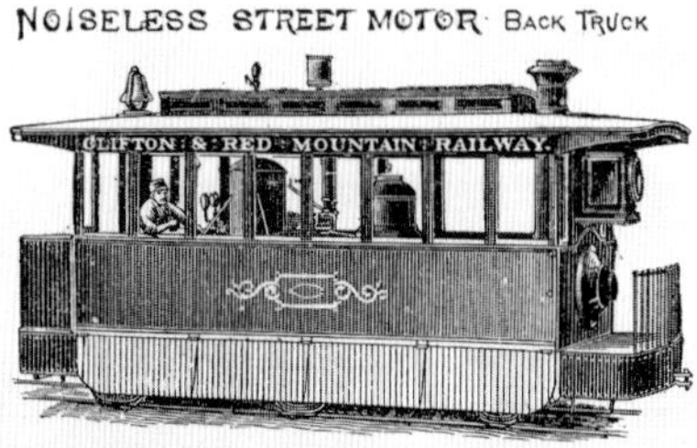

These Motors have been designed especially for hauling street cars, either through cities or on suburban extensions.

The fuel used is Anthracite Coal or Coke, so that no smoke is made. This style is used where it is necessary to distribute the weight of Motor.

They are all fitted with noiseless exhaust, and have muffled safety valves and cylinder drain cocks.

NOTE.—This Motor has the entrance in the rear, which can be reached by stepping from platform of first car, or it can be built with doors on the side if so desired.

STREET RAILROAD LOCOMOTIVE—WITH BACK-TRUCK AND TANK IN REAR.

Cylinder Dia. and Stroke in inches.	Driver Dia. in inches.	Rigid Wheel Base.	Total Wheel Base.	Water Capacity of Tank.	Weight in Working Order.	Hauling Capacity in Tons of 2,000 Pounds.
8x12	30	4.0	8.6	250 gallons.	20,000 pounds.	325
9x14	33	4.6	9.6	300 "	24,000 "	400
10x14	36	4.6	9.6	350 "	28,000 "	490
10x16	36	5.3	12.4	350 "	32,000 "	600

Advertisement, Richmond Locomotive and Machine Works, street railroad locomotive, with back-track and tank in rear, circa 1889. *John H. White Jr. Railroad Reference Collection, Archives Center, National Museum of American History, Smithsonian Institution.*

to support the endeavor; no meter was used to gauge city water usage at Bryan's facility so as not to "impose any hardship upon the Locomotive Works."[219] In the fall of 1900, when employment at the Works reached nearly 2,500, a new boiler shop neared completion; south of the erecting department, this new single-story boiler shop reached a height of 60 feet, a length of 435 feet and a width of 70 feet. Three sets of windows provided light to the 38,000 square footage of floor space the building offered, with the entire eastern end supporting a riveter based on one located at New York's Schenectady Locomotive Works and capable of pressures of up to 125 tons. Three hydraulic cranes, one able to lift 50 tons and the other two 25 tons each, could be used to transfer the massive locomotive boilers the shop produced. The building's northern side featured a loading platform for raw materials, and the entire structure was designed in such a way that raw materials could easily arrive at one end and follow seamlessly along the production line until the finished product emerged from the other. Punch machines, drills, shears, a hydraulic press capable of applying 125 tons of pressure, and rolls for producing angle bars were among the machinery in the new building, in which five fires were constantly kept alight to allow for the heating and manipulation of iron and steel.[220] The need for workers expanded as well, with the company placing ads seeking no fewer than 25 "first-class" carpenters, likely for work in the pattern shop.[221] The new boiler shop was completed just in time, as new orders continued to arrive; in January 1900, the Wabash

Representatives of the Richmond Locomotive and Machine Works at the Exposition Universelle, Paris, France, 1900. *Nathan Vernon Madison.*

Railroad placed an order for 34 2-6-0 engines (commonly referred to as a Mogul type locomotive), 6 4-6-0 passenger engines, 6 4-4-2 Atlantic types and 4 0-4-0 switching engines, for a total of 50 engines in all.[222] The company's charter was altered to allow for a rise in capital stock, from $2.5 million to $4.5 million; charter amendments also came with a name change, as the firm now chose to be known simply as the Richmond Locomotive Works.[223] Costs relating to the general maintenance of the plant had risen, from $42,955.36 in 1896 to $72,860.12 in 1899; those same years saw an increase in fuel consumption in the boiler and erecting shops, as well as the various forges and foundries across the site, rising from $28,078 to $50,840.41, respectively. Resultingly, with an increase in workmen, labor costs rose from $46,548.72 in 1896 to $82,444.36 in 1899.[224]

4

THE AMERICAN LOCOMOTIVE COMPANY—RICHMOND WORKS

1901–1914

In 1903, the Richmond Chamber of Commerce published what can only be described as a panegyric to Richmond's financial and manufacturing sectors:

> *Richmond, Virginia, picturesque capital of the Old Dominion, city on the James! City of checkered fortune; Revolutionary role; bare forty years ago the seat and scene, and gage, of many a bloody action of four years' Civil War! Haunt of Smith and Pocahontas, Byrd, Patrick Henry, Jefferson, Monroe, Marshall; stage of names and memories perennial and glorious, "dear to every American heart!"*[225]

Overall, Virginia was 9th in manufacturing in the United States as the Civil War began; by 1899, it had dropped to 22nd.[226] Virginia saw a 30.4 percent increase in its total population between 1850 and 1900 and a concurrent rise in manufactory workers by 150 percent.[227] The number of wage earners within Richmond increased, as its population more than doubled from 37,910 in 1860 to a little over 85,000 on the eve of the twentieth century. Despite such state and citywide augmentations, Richmond's industrial standing was being overtaken by other cities.[228] Michael B. Chesson has argued, quite convincingly, that Richmond's decline as an industrial hub in the latter years of the nineteenth century, insofar as national comparisons are concerned, stemmed from a retrenchment of conservative business and social views on the part of Richmond's ruling class that stifled economic and industrial growth. Further, other cities and states simply conducted themselves better when attempting to compete nationally, as evidenced by Birmingham, Alabama's growth into the metallurgic capital of the South, a title once held by Richmond for decades prior. The number of manufacturing establishments in Virginia grew substantially between 1880 and 1900, and while some of these can be attributed to Richmond, new industrial growth in areas such as Roanoke and the shipyards of Newport News contributed heavily, as well.

However, this is not to say that Richmond had ceased to be a potent and powerful industrial force at the dawn of the twentieth century, for this period undoubtedly witnessed one of, if not the, greatest concentration of large-scale industrial and manufacturing concerns the city had ever seen to that point. Collectively, Richmond's leading flour mills—Dunlop, Haxall, and Gallego—were capable of producing 3,500 barrels a day in 1890, with succeeding years witnessing some of Gallego's highest-recorded exports.[229] From humble beginnings in 1871 within the remnants of the former Libby Prison, the Richmond Cedar Works grew into one of the region's premier industries, eventually occupying a 12-acre complex near Rocketts Landing along the James River, the largest woodworking facility of the era. The Cedar Works employed approximately 1,500 workmen by 1900 producing everything from wooden washing machines and butter churns to simple buckets and clothes pins; by 1903, the firm operated branches in New York, Baltimore, Chicago, and several other major cities.[230] The Tredegar Iron Works was experiencing one of its most profitable phases, as was the Old Dominion Iron and Nail Works on nearby Belle Isle, which, in October 1887, became one of the earliest iron works in the South to install Bessemer convertors.[231] The Southern Stove Works, founded in 1880 by William J. Loth and originally located at 1422 and 1424 East Cary Street, following a brief slump in the late nineteenth century, had rebounded and took advantage of a boom in stoves sales throughout the country with a new, massive factory at the intersection of Leigh and Hermitage Streets in 1902, which included a direct connection to the RF&P line.[232] Approximately 900 million cigarettes, around one-third of the cigarettes sold in the United States a year, were produced annually in the first years of the twentieth century by the firm of Allen & Ginter, a subsidiary of the American Tobacco Company.[233] R.H. Bosher's Sons Carriage Manufactory (9th Street and Cary), the Watt Plow Company (15th and Franklin), L.H. Jenkins' New Book Manufactory (Broad and Allison), the Albemarle Paper Manufacturing Company (off Tredegar Street), H.W. Rountree & Brothers Trunk and Bag Company (201 to 217

North 14th Street), John R. Johnson & Co. Car Axle Works (on Maury Street): these and scores of others dotted the Richmond cityscape.

Richmond's growth in this period also owed a great deal to the railroad lines and numerous shipping depots across the city that made it a regional entrepôt; in 1891 alone, this trade generated $36 million.[234] The 1890s may have been the pinnacle of Richmond's status as a manufacturing center—over 21,000 individual workers employed across 783 manufacturers in 1890—and soon, the number of works, employees employed in such fields, and the revenue generated by their labor was soon overshadowed by other locales.[235] Again, it should not be assumed that Richmond did not continue to be a strong voice in southern and American industry. In 1903, the Richmond Chamber of Commerce estimated that the roughly 800—large and small—industrial establishments in the city (as well as neighboring Manchester, which Richmond would annex in 1910) employed approximately 18,000 workers and could boast of over $30 million in products manufactured, the purchasing power of over $1 billion in 2022.[236]

On May 7, 1901, it was announced that the Richmond Locomotive Works had been sold for $3 million (approximately $104 million in 2022) to a Chicago businessman named Joseph Leiter, acting on behalf of a holding company, the International Power Company. The International Power Company was led by three men: Leiter, along with fellow investors Pliny Fisk, of the railroad financing firm Harvey Fisk & Sons, and Joseph Hoadley, a New England financier. The trio eventually gained control over eight of the era's locomotive producers: Providence-based Rhode Island Locomotive Works; the Cooke Locomotive Works of Paterson, New Jersey; the Schenectady Locomotive Works in New York State; the Brooks Locomotive Works of Dunkirk, New York; the Dickson Locomotive Works in Scranton; the Manchester Locomotive Works of Manchester, New Hampshire; the Pittsburgh Locomotive Works; and the Richmond Locomotive Works.

As of June 24, Richmond, and the seven other locomotive works under the Broadley-Fisk-Leiter banner, had officially merged to form a single company: the American Locomotive Company. With an authorized capital stock of $50 million, the American Locomotive Company, or ALCO, was formed in hopes of combatting what many saw to be a monopoly on the part of the Baldwin Locomotive Works of Philadelphia, which since its founding in 1825 had grown to become the largest single producer of locomotives in the country, having cornered 39 percent of the domestic locomotive market by itself for most of the 1890s, 946 engines constructed in 1899 alone.[237] The president of the new enterprise was Samuel R.

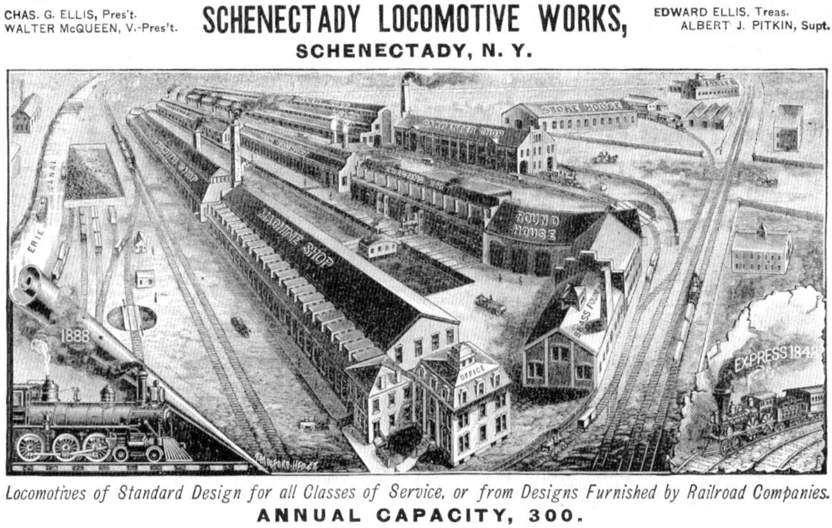

Advertisement, Schenectady Locomotive Works, circa 1888. *Nathan Vernon Madison.*

Callaway, formerly president of the New York Central Railroad. ALCO was also obligated to pay principal and accrued interest on all mortgage bonds issued by several of the predecessor firms, including two from Richmond: Tanner & Delaney Engine Company 7 percent gold bonds, which were scheduled to mature on July 1, 1904, as well as 6 percent gold bonds from April 1, 1889, issued by the Richmond Locomotive Works, set to mature on April 1, 1929.[238] The new American Locomotive Company ended its first full fiscal year of operations on sound financial footing; having expended a little over $1.6 million in repairs, additional land, machine tools, and upgrades to its constituent plants, the firm recorded gross earnings of over $26 million, allowing for a 7 percent dividend on preferred stock equaling $1.75 million and a surplus of well over $1.2 million.[239] The following fiscal year, ending on June 30, 1903, proved even better: $33 million in earnings and a surplus of $3 million.[240]

ALCO's origins actually date to a decade before the company's formation to a rather informal assembly of locomotive luminaries hosted by the Rhode Island Locomotive Works' President Charles Felix Mason in 1889 at New York's famed Delmonico restaurant—a gathering that, by 1891, had evolved into an organization called the American Locomotive Manufacturer's Association. By June 7, 1894, when the Association held its annual meeting in Richmond, at which William R. Trigg was elected second vice-president of the group, its roster was composed of 11 members, seven of the eight firms that would later join under the ALCO banner (sans Manchester), as well as the Baldwin Works; the Rogers Locomotive Works, of Paterson; the Porter Locomotive Works of Pittsburgh; and the Grant Locomotive Works of Chicago. The Richmond meeting was held at the Commonwealth Club, following a tour of the Richmond Works as well as brief tours of Richmond landmarks, including the Virginia Capitol, the former Confederate Presidential Mansion, St. Paul's Church, and the newly constructed Richmond City Hall. After official business had been addressed, the party was treated to a cruise down the James River to Dutch Gap. Among the invited guests were Alexander Delaney and Tredegar's Edward R. Archer; upon returning to Richmond, a grand dinner was held, once again at the Commonwealth Club. The following morning, accommodations having been provided at the homes of the Richmond Works' officers, private meetings were again held, at both Bryan's Laburnum estate as well as at Ginter's Westbrook.[241] The ensuing years saw fluctuations among the association's membership, with several plants closing or leaving the organization, most notably the Baldwin

Advertisement, American Locomotive Company, circa 1905. *Nathan Vernon Madison.*

Locomotive Works, until eventually the remaining members, one by one, with the addition of New Hampshire's Manchester Works, were combined to create ALCO.

Bryan's son recounted that his father believed he did not have much of a choice whether he would join this syndicate or not. Consolidation was the order of the day throughout American industries, and Bryan apparently felt that inaction on his part would result in the Richmond Works being "crushed" between the industry leader, Baldwin, and the newly established ALCO. As was a constant throughout the life of the company, under whatever name it held at the time, indebtedness was a relentless concern, and the younger Bryan recounted that the Works "owed 'a slue of money.'" It was perhaps this concern that preoccupied Bryan one night in 1898, when he confessed, "Son, things are looking pretty bad for me at the Locomotive Works," before abruptly changing the topic and mood with a joke about moving back to Fluvanna if things happened to fall apart in Richmond.[242] Nonetheless, Bryan, who was the largest shareholder at the time, did stand his ground when he believed the syndicate offered him less than justified and was rewarded with the difference; on the other hand, his business acumen failed him somewhat when he neglected, unlike the owners of the other plants, to request an additional sum for all the small tools on hand, replying when this was brought to his attention that "it never occurred to me to charge for them."[243]

The creation of ALCO was just one instance of what Oliver Zunz has labeled an "organizational revolution" within the United States' business and industrial sectors in the late nineteenth and early twentieth centuries.[244] Not only were many independent companies bought and consolidated into larger, national firms, such as the Morgan interests' purchase of the Carnegie Steel Company and other businesses to create the behemoth U.S. Steel in 1901, but there were also internal changes, as a new managerial class, educated in rational business methodology, began to assume positions in and ever-increasing power over the day-to-day operations of many firms. The growth of America's railroads coincidently helped fuel this change. As railroads expanded, an ever-larger bureaucracy was obligatory in order to manage a business rife with complexities that required near control of, or at the very least intelligent management regarding, a variety of factors, from finance, to customer service, to mechanical engineering—all were needed to function in concert with one another. Even time itself was bent to the needs of the railroad, with the time zones in use in America today having much of their origins in attempts to set a standard time for railways across the continent. The management of departments that arose out of necessity in the case of the railroads provided something of a blueprint to the managerial and leadership structures the nation's large corporations would inevitably adopt.[245] ALCO was built on this evolving, rationalized approach to business management from its inception. Its first annual report states that, among the benefits expected from amalgamation was the interchange of ideas as to shop practices gained from the various composite companies' experiences, as well as work toward, as much as possible, the standardization of the locomotive-manufacturing process. The directors understood that far more could be achieved by examining and systematizing their own processes in an analytical manner: "It has been the aim of the directors to increase the company's profits through the lowering of manufacturing and administrative cost rather than by increase in the selling price of locomotives." This systemization of processes filtered down to the smallest of details; prior to 1901, locomotive purchases at the Richmond Works were jotted down in a traditional ledger and kept among the rest of "the books." Following the merger, all orders were recorded on official ALCO letterhead, with standardized formatting and cost tallies, carbon-copied and appearing, truth be told, far more professional and organized.

Such acquisitions also illustrated a change in the role of the city's societal elites. The growth of Richmond industry in the 1850s that culminated in it being the industrial center of the late Confederacy was largely overseen by a relatively small group of elites, a cadre of "self-confident, forward-looking bourgeoisie" composed of the area's leading landowners, bankers, and merchants.[246] Men of this generation, rather grayed by the 1900s, were still considered the pillars of their community, their prominence only heightened by their service during the war, a glamorization the Lost Cause was beginning to ensconce in popular imagination. Joseph Bryan, William Trigg, Lewis Ginter, James Dooley, and Archer Anderson were all young men at the time of the war but nonetheless shared in the same heightened status as their predecessors in Richmond industry, for much the same reason—"good" family names and service to "the Cause." However, such local prominence began to hold less sway at the Richmond Locomotive Works as of 1901. Gone were the days of the Works belonging to a handful of Richmond's privileged, whose prominence and place in society were largely owed to a South no longer in existence, despite their wishes to the contrary. The Works was now part of a sprawling national, multistate corporation, with its leadership in New York; this leadership took no particular interest in the regional pride and local concerns that had been first and foremost on the minds of its previous stewards. While many Richmond businesses, such as the Tredegar Iron Works, the Richmond Cedar Works, Albemarle Paper Manufacturing, and others were able to retain their individual existences for decades to come, the Richmond Locomotive Works, largely due to its nature as a producer of capital goods, could not escape consolidation. The Works, however, was not the sole Richmond concern to succumb to this nationwide, organizational drive. Founded by James Buchanan Duke, the American Tobacco Company was a conglomeration of several formerly independent tobacco producers, of which Richmond's Allen & Ginter, a powerhouse in the tobacco industry and the first to include baseball cards in cigarette packages, was largely coerced into joining in 1890 following Buchanan's exclusive licensing of James Bonsack's cigarette-rolling machine, with Ginter reduced to the role of a director.[247]

As was the case with the other presidents of ALCO's constituent firms, Joseph Bryan gained a seat on the board of the new corporation and retained local control of what was now the Richmond Branch of the American Locomotive Company as its managing director, with a monthly salary of $833.32, or the purchasing power of approximately $29,000 in 2022. General superintendent H.A. Gillis's salary was $500 ($17,000 in 2022); superintendent of the construction department F.A. Haughton, $333.38 ($11,600); mechanical engineer C.J. Mellin, $250 ($8,700); and C.K. Lassiter, now a traveling clerk, $125 ($4,350).[248] It is important to remember that while managers, engineers, and machinists certainly held positions of import at the Locomotive Works, there was a rather large clerical staff (approximately 60 strong in 1901) who contributed just as much to the successful daily functioning of the plant. Such individuals included: Local Purchasing Agent W.R. Williams, with a monthly salary of $150 (approximately $5,238 in 2022); Pay Clerk J.H. Vaughan, $70 ($2,444); Superintendent Stenographer J.L. Phippen, $65 ($2,270); Store Room Clerk W.H. Miles, $60 ($2,095); Telegraph Operator A.O. Osterbind, $50 ($1,746); Mail Clerk J.S. Wakler, $35 ($1,222); Janitor Pen Bryant, $32.50 ($1,135); Pay Clerk H.P. Eustace, $20 ($698); and Telephone Boy Charles Boeck, $5 ($175). During its first full three years under ALCO management, 1902 to 1905, the Richmond Works shipped 515 locomotives; from 1905 to 1908, that rose to 723. During those six years, 222 locomotives went to the C&O, 189 to the Baltimore & Ohio Railroad, and 190 to Bryan's Southern Railway.

Bryan's long association with the Works in one capacity or another, combined with his management abilities as demonstrated—not so much by his presidency of the Works (which was relatively brief) but rather in his

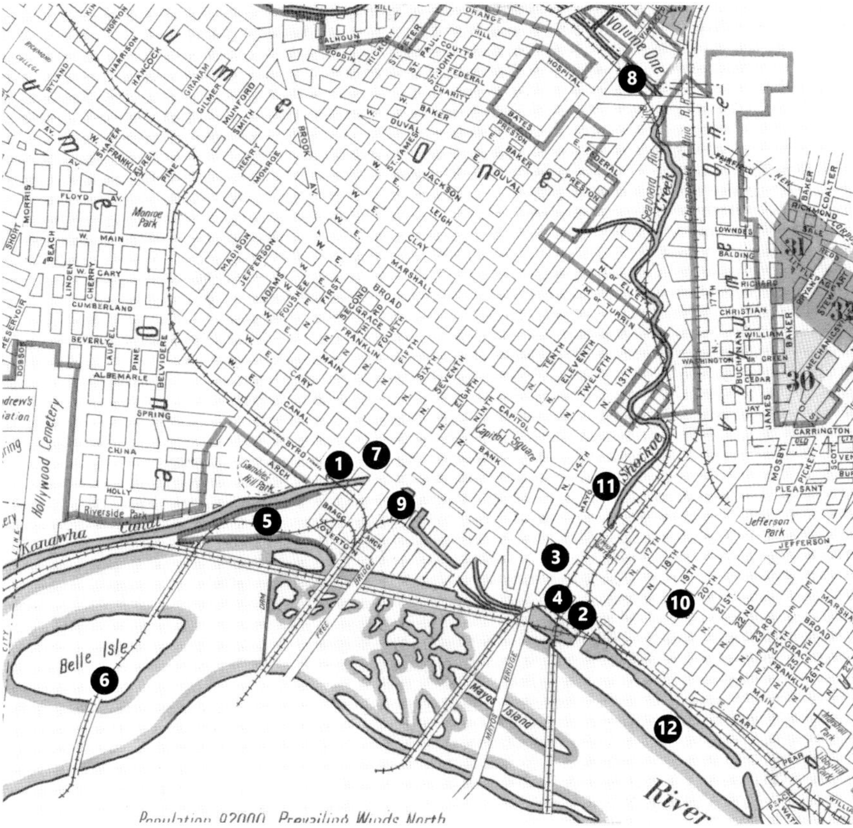

Sanborn Insurance Map of Richmond, with locations of engine manufactories and related establishments throughout Richmond's history. *Nathan Vernon Madison. Original Map, Library of Congress, Geography and Map Division, Sanborn Maps Collection.*

1. D.J. Burr
2. Shockoe Manufacturing Company / Talbott & Brother
3. Philip Rahm / Eagle Foundry
4. Burr & Ettenger
5. Tredegar Iron Works
6. Old Dominion Iron and Nail Works
7. Metropolitan Iron Works / Tanner & Delaney Engine Company
8. Tanner & Delaney Engine Company / Richmond Locomotive Works / ALCO Richmond
9. Richmond Iron Works, first location
10. Ettenger & Edmonds
11. Richmond Iron Works, second location
12. William R. Trigg Shipbuilding Company

newspaper, iron, and railroad interests—was certainly a benefit to ALCO. Bryan's role at Sloss-Sheffield as well as his influence on the boards of several regional railroads allowed for insider information that could prove invaluable. "As to the rumored order by the Southern Railway for 20 switchers with the Baldwin Company, I can hardly think that is true," Bryan wrote to ALCO president Callaway on December 28, 1903, in response to intra-industry rumors. "I expect to be in New York on Tuesday, the 5th of January to attend a meeting of the Southern directors, and I will come and see you."[249] Bryan's presence could also prove beneficial in easily resolving local affairs, such as his efforts that same month to lower ALCO Richmond's power bill, following the Virginia Passenger & Power Company's announcement that it planned to raise rates from 1½ to 2½ ¢ per kilowatt-hour. Bryan was able to negotiate several options, including the possibility of renting outright a new power station recently erected on Brown's Island, all to ALCO's benefit.[250] He even aided ALCO management in ways not directly tied to the company itself, such as providing detailed information regarding the finances of Sloss-Sheffield to several ALCO executives who had shown interest in becoming shareholders of the firm in the summer of 1903.[251]

Bryan now occupied an interesting position at ALCO; no longer the president of an independent company, he was now a subordinate to others, and instances of friction within this new relationship are perceptible in remaining records. Writing on March 27, 1903, to C.E. Patterson, ALCO controller in New York, following the parent company's apparent attempts to lower the compensation allotted to local counsels, and thus curb their use in favor of lawyers hired by the New York office to represent all of ALCO, Bryan argued for the retainment of the firm's longtime legal representative, one Murray McGuire:

> *Mr. McGuire has well earned his compensation, and that while for some weeks or even a month his services may not be required, yet he may be engaged for days altogether on a matter that would be worth all he is paid for months. If we give up Mr. McGuire entirely, we would have no one to represent us in petty misdemeanors, fights and larcenies, which will continue to occur. I am clearly of the opinion that it would be unwise to abandon the services of regular consul.*[252]

McGuire was indeed retained by ALCO Richmond and was representing the company's interests as late as 1938. In other instances, Bryan spoke openly of what he considered the imperious nature of his relationship to

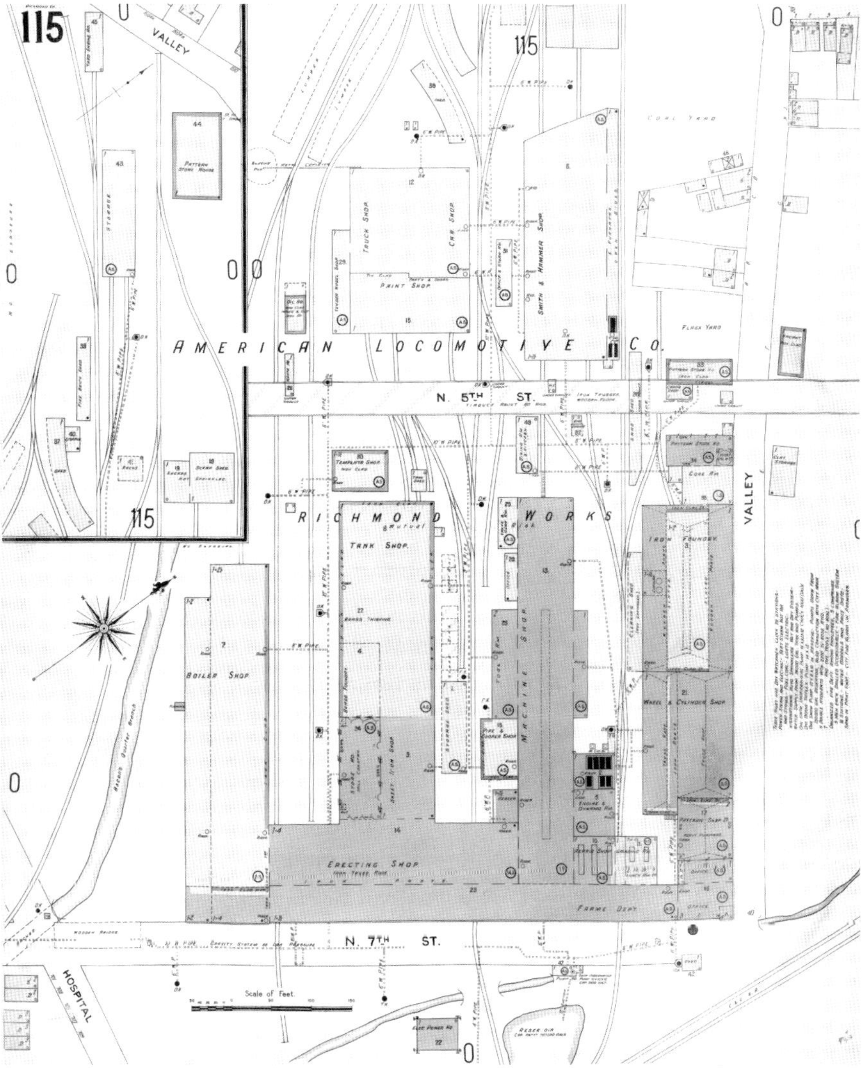

American Locomotive Company—Richmond Works, 1905, Sanborn Insurance Maps. *Library of Congress, Geography and Map Division, Sanborn Maps Collection.*

ALCO's leadership. In writing to Reverend Beverley D. Tucker to make known his inability to attend the next meeting of the Episcopal Church's Commission for Work Among Colored People, Bryan complained, "This morning I received a letter from Mr. Callaway, president of the company. Of course, my engagement with them is of a peremptory kind and I must wait to see them….I have only a name to live without any power."[253] Bryan would also argue in favor of workers that he believed ALCO's management did not fully appreciate. When in December 1903 a cut to the payroll department would have resulted in the dismissal of a longtime employee, Bryan wrote to C.B. Denny, ALCO treasurer: "I would be glad if some arrangement can be made whereby Mr. Ferguson can be offered occupation with a salary appropriate to the change of conditions.…He has been with the company for about eighteen years and has been faithful and accurate, and in the days of my own financing, which are happily passed, he was really invaluable.…It would be a gratifying recognition of long and good service." Ensuing correspondences confirms that Ferguson's position was indeed retained.[254] On May 28, 1906, Bryan wrote to Waldo H. Marshall, ALCO's third president, requesting that a portion of his yearly salary be subtracted and given instead to a workman whom he believed deserved a higher pay; in 1907, during the heights of that year's economic panic when the ALCO leadership in Schenectady decided to reduce salaries of workmen at the Richmond Branch, Bryan wrote in response, "You are now paying me $10,000 a year as managing director: I don't need it and I am not sure that I earn it. What I wish you to do is to take my adjusted salary and divide it among the boys here; they need it, and I want them to have it."[255]

Healthcare at the Works

Bryan's missives to Patterson regarding legal counsel are noteworthy also, as they relate to concerns regarding workplace safety. "You will remember," Bryan wrote to Patterson, "that we had 194 accidents at the locomotive works last year, and we have several suits now pending against us." Bryan's opinions on workers' healthcare were expressed during a conversation with his son (whom he would often jokingly refer to as a "half-baked Socialist" due to his political views), during an afternoon walk about Laburnum in October 1908.

> *Yesterday we broke a hundred-thousand-dollar machine for forming boilers. The cost of that machine will have to be figured in the price of future sales, and this is proper; but when a man is broken by an accident he is thrown on the scrap heap.…This is all wrong. The society in whose service a man is maimed or killed owes that man and his family reparation.…If you want to call me a Socialist, too, I'll have to let you.*[256]

The issue of workplace injuries and deaths was a constant at the Works, as it was at any similar facility. Every day, a myriad of potential calamities faced workmen, everything from standard finger-mashing and fragments of iron striking workmen's eyes to men crushed to death by falling machinery. On August 16, 1900, German immigrant Henry Ganzert, an employee of several years, was severely injured when a 40-pound hammer hit him square on the head, crushing his skull. While Bryan maintained the services of a dedicated surgeon, Dr. Gills of the Richmond Ambulance Corps, in the event of workplace injury, Dr. Stuart McGuire, son of famed Richmond surgeon Dr. Hunter Holmes McGuire, was called and operated as best he could, attempting to remove shards of skull embedded in his patient's brain. Ganzert, however, died several days later on the 20th.[257] On November 30, 1900, William Golden, an African American resident of Manchester employed at the Works, suffered a smashed foot on account of dislodged piping. And in many instances, as Joseph Bryan alluded to in his correspondence, workmen did take their employer to court; a laborer named Joseph Rankin sued the company in October 1900 following an injury he sustained while on the job, and the courts awarded him $5,000 in restitution.[258] Injury or death could even claim those simply visiting the facility. On March 7, 1900, during a tour of the plant with her family, twelve-year-old Susie Gibson's hair became entangled in a belt, whipping her violently about the machine to which it was attached and resulting in several life-threatening injuries—while she initially showed signs of recovery, she unfortunately died of her wounds several days later.[259]

In 1889, the Beneficial Society of the Richmond Locomotive and Machine Works was organized. The society's relief fund, which was subsidized by $0.30 deducted weekly from a member's wages, provided for workers in the event of illness, injury or death: "temporary disablement from sickness or accident shall entitle each member in good standing to a weekly allowance of $3 for a period not exceeding six months from date of disability."[260] For workers who earned less than $3.00 per week, both deductions and benefits were halved. In the event of permanent injury or death, members were obligated to donate $0.25 each, which would be pooled and provided to the worker, or widow. The plan obviously enjoyed the support of management, as the company had two representatives on the society's five-member board, and the Works itself agreed to match contributions collected that first year and presumably in years thereafter. In 1889, $762 was paid out to eligible workers; of that, the families of four workers who succumbed to various illnesses were provided $154, collectively.[261] In January 1889, the number of enrolled workers was 170; by year's end, that number had risen 55 percent, to 264, with $1,836.58 in funds on hand. In a plea to prospective members, the chairman of the society wrote, "I cannot urge enough upon you all to interest yourselves in the workings of this Society, for you cannot tell at what moment any one of you may be called upon to partake of its benefits."[262]

While clearly established in good faith, such a program did not adequately meet the needs of workmen, an issue Joseph Bryan attempted to address following the ALCO acquisition. On March 23, 1903, Bryan began a correspondence with Dr. Ennion Gifford Williams of Richmond's Memorial Hospital; at the time of these dispatches, the hospital, located at the corner of 12th and Broad Streets, just northeast of the Governor's Mansion, was still under construction. The 64 private- and 124 ward-bed facility did not open until several months later, on July 27.[263] Bryan's proposal to Williams (who, in 1908, was named the first state health commissioner of Virginia) was quite progressive for the time. He proposed a system wherein the company paid a lump monthly sum (anywhere between $500 and $2,000) to ensure that any and all injured workmen at the Richmond Branch were treated fully and completely, either at their home or, if need be, in the hospital's beds. "I will want the best surgical attention and I will want at least first class ward room treatment for the patient," Bryan explained. "We are working in all, night and day force, about 2,300 men, of about two-thirds worked in the day time. The majority of accidents are injuries to heads, hands and feet." Bryan desired that the men be provided "full hospital care and all surgical attention necessary until they are well able to leave the hospital" and the same at their place of residence, if so desired and approved by the hospital staff.[264] This is an unfortunate example wherein existing records provide no satisfactory resolution, as neither the few remaining Bryan letterbooks and Richmond Works records, nor the surviving archives of the Memorial Hospital, reveal whether such a plan ever came to fruition. However, a 1905 article regarding Edward Hildebrand, a workman seriously injured on the job, recounts how he was convalescing at Richmond's Virginia Hospital (1010 Floyd Avenue) in a ward "set aside and devoted to such as become injured at the Locomotive Works," suggesting that Bryan's plan was initiated, perhaps not at Memorial, but elsewhere.[265]Also in March 1903, Bryan introduced an unemployment and life insurance program for ALCO Richmond employees, in a similar vein as the Beneficial Society of years past. Under Bryan's plan, a penny from every dollar earned would be deducted from every enrollee's pay, and in the event of illness or injury, half of his regular wages would be paid to him during his convalescence; in the unfortunate case of death, a sizable amount would be provided for funeral expenses.[266]

One concept of Bryan's that we know was successful came in early July 1904: a full-service, 24-hour restaurant along the western edge of the Works, to provide workmen with fresh, substantive meals, regardless of the time of day. For between $0.10 to $0.20, workers could enjoy a meal (breakfast, lunch, or dinner)—and a complementary cigar, to boot—with clean and efficient service thanks to the "corps of quick, affable waiters." Workers could purchase books from the company for the price of $1.00 that contained a multitude of tickets valued at $0.01 each, thereby allotting the men a voucher system by which they could purchase meals at the restaurant at a cost far below most other similar establishments in the city. The restaurant was not operated by the Works itself but rather by W.M. Crease, to whom the company rented space, power, and other amenities. The restaurant was reportedly capable of feeding 1,000 at a time, which necessitated Crease procuring his meat and produce at wholesale and keeping his soup tanks, 40 gallons worth, full round the clock. Workers' choices included: "Hamburg steak, 3¢; Roast ribs of prime beef, 3¢; liver and onion, 3¢; finest fried potatoes, 3¢; steamed new potatoes, 3¢; steamed new cabbage, 3¢; stewed squash, 3¢; vegetable soup, 3¢; string beans, 3¢; eggs with ham to order, 5¢; tenderloin steak, 10¢; ice cream, 3¢; plum pudding, 3¢; pie (all kinds), 3¢; milk, 2¢; butter, 1¢; coffee, 2¢; lemonade, 2¢; bananas, 3¢; plums, 3¢."

"I got the idea by serving as a member of the Board of Directors of the penitentiary," Bryan explained.

> *Here we purchased all the supplies in bulk, and at the closest wholesale prices. I was astounded one day at the very low prices, at which we were getting what proved to be a good article of toasted coffee. I took a handful of it home, and found it was all right.... I commenced to consider if there was any reason why our men at the Locomotive Works could not be given the benefit of these low prices, and at the same be furnished with hot meals at lunch hour.... Talk about your social problems. I believe this is one of them, for after all, they are but those questions which relate to the comfort and well being of any considerable number of the human family. I am delighted with the operation of the new restaurant system, and I believe it is a great reform.*[267]

A *Richmond Times-Dispatch* reporter observing the diner's operations noted that workers of all stripes partook of the restaurant's offerings, with many of the unmarried, younger workmen relying on the Works for all of their meals; one longtime, widowed employee, along with his several small children, were each provided three full meals a day at the ALCO Richmond lunchroom. The venture proved so successful that the pattern was followed at fellow ALCO works in Dunkirk, as well as at two new ALCO acquisitions: the Montreal Locomotive Works in Quebec (purchased by ALCO in 1904), and the Rogers Locomotive Works of Paterson, New Jersey (acquired in 1905). Even the central plant at Schenectady reportedly followed suit with its own version.

A regular event that was inaugurated under Bryan's tenure on June 21, 1902—although his role in its creation is uncertain—was an annual one-day excursion for workers and their families to Buckroe Beach on the Chesapeake Bay, slightly north of Fort Monroe in the city of Hampton. This holiday was funded in part by the Works itself, in conjunction with the International Association of Machinists' Richmond Branch and other unions.[268] The outing, with anywhere between 2,000 and 4,000 beachgoers depending on the year, all of whom were carried to Hampton via the C&O Railroad free of charge, was promoted as a family-friendly undertaking, with "rowdyism a stranger" as "everything to eat and drink to make the crowd merry will be provided, except of course that there will be no intoxicants."[269] Contests and events included: a prettiest baby competition, an apple eating contest, a sack race, a 100-yard dash, a three-legged race, and catch the greasy pig, among others. Attendees also enjoyed baseball games, with the 1902 and 1903 matches between Manchester's own "Blue Jeans" and the Locomotive Works' "Choo Choos," both resulting in resounding victories for the former.[270] Bryan was evidently pleased with the success of such events. "I send you herewith a newspaper account of the Locomotive excursion on Last Saturday," Bryan wrote to President Callaway following the 1903 event. "I wish to add my own testimony that a more perfectly agreeable and satisfactory entertainment of the kind was never had in America....It was altogether a most inspiring and gratifying experience to see so many well-dressed, well-behaved happy people from infants in arms to that of the three score years and ten." Never one to lose sight of a good business angle, however, Bryan closed his letter by adding "I really believe that if that story was written up as it might be, it would be a notable contribution to the labor literature of the day."[271] At the 1910 Buckroe Beach outing, William Brooks, with a total of 43 years on the job, was recognized for holding the longest unbroken tenure at the Richmond Works.

Alabama Great Southern No. 185, 1902, 4-6-0. *John H. White Jr. Railroad Reference Collection, Archives Center, National Museum of American History, Smithsonian Institution.*

In a 20-man tug of war between blacksmiths and boilermakers, the latter were the victors; accolades for the largest family in attendance were given to S.H. Webb and his 11 children. The award for Fat Man's 50-Yard Race went to all 260 pounds of one John Martin, and Robert M. Straer was recognized for his achievement as ALCO Richmond's Baldest Man. The event was observed nearly every year until 1927. The *Times* announcement of the inaugural 1902 excursion states that the trip was open only to the Works' white employees; whether this changed as ALCO Richmond's directives increasingly originated from the New York office in succeeding years is unknown, as no further notices make mention of it.[272]

The absorption of the Richmond Works into ALCO allowed for vast improvements to the facilities, including a newly expanded (at the cost of approximately $100,000), 303-by-72-foot erecting shop, with a 120-ton crane, long sought after by Superintendent Gillis.[273] Such expansions allowed for both more orders to be taken, as well as for the construction of some of the largest locomotives ALCO Richmond would produce in later years, such as the 14, 214-ton 2-6-6-2 compound locomotives shipped to the C&O in 1914 and the 16, 248-ton 2-8-8-2 engines put to work on the Seaboard Air Line in 1918. These engines were known as Mallet types; the Mallet was an articulated locomotive, meaning it had two sets of driving wheels, one of which could move independently of the locomotive's frame, a particularly helpful advantage on routes with formidable curves. In reference to the 2-8-8-2 notation, this identifies the engine as having two leading wheels, one set of eight driving wheels (the independent set), a second set of eight driving wheels (the stationary set), and two trailing wheels.

ARTICULATED COMPOUND LOCOMOTIVES

Fig. 25 The First Mallet Articulated Compound Locomotive Built in America

BUILT FOR THE BALTIMORE AND OHIO RAILROAD BY THE AMERICAN LOCOMOTIVE COMPANY

Gage of track	4 ft. 8½ in.	Outside diameter of tubes	2¼ in.
Diameter of cylinders	h.p. 20 in.; l.p. 32 in.	Length of tubes	21 ft.
Stroke of piston	32 in.	Driving wheel base	30 ft. 8 in.
Diameter of driving wheels	56 in.	Rigid wheel base	10 ft.
Outside diameter of boiler at front end	84 in.	Total weight in working order	334 500 lb.
Working pressure	235 lb.	Weight on driving wheels	334 500 lb.
Length of firebox	108 in.	Tractive power	71 500 lb.
Width of firebox	96 in.	Tractive power working simple	91 000 lb.
Number of tubes	436	Factor of adhesion	4.67

Mallet articulated compound locomotive, of the type manufactured at ALCO Richmond. *John H. White Jr. Railroad Reference Collection, Archives Center, National Museum of American History, Smithsonian Institution.*

By 1905, the eastern face of the Works bordered 7th Street, while its northern boundary remained Valley Road. The basic *E* shape as constructed under Tanner & Delaney remained, albeit expanded. The dimensions of the iron truss-roofed erecting shop were enlarged to allow for the incorporation of a frame shop directly behind. The three original prongs of the *E* were augmented laterally to house an even larger iron foundry, machine shop (assimilating the entirety of the former carpenter shop), and boiler shop, while an additional fourth (between the machine and boiler shops), containing tank and sheet iron shops, was present by 1905. These structures were enhanced not only to provide more expansive working spaces but also so as to incorporate related operations. The machine shop contained its own dedicated tool room, pipe and cooper room, and office, while the tank and sheet iron shops featured an internal brass foundry. Additional buildings were added at the end of the iron foundry, including a pattern storage shop and core room. A short distance westward, across 5th Street (which extended over the Works via a viaduct), were several other additions, including a massive smith and hammer shop, as well as an equally large building that housed truck, car, paint, and tender wheel shops; scattered across the entire site were various scrap and storage sheds. A large coal yard for powering the Works' many furnaces lay directly north of the smith and hammer shop. A 24,000-gallon water tank on-site was joined by direct connections to the city's water system as well as a reservoir directly across 7th Street to provide water to both the

Work's sprinkler system and the 19 fire hydrants spread across the grounds. The Richmond Works also operated its own fire department, three companies, each composed of nine employees, who performed regular drills to maintain readiness. Internal and city fire alarms; 18 water stations, complete with barrels and pails; and copious amounts of sand in the paint shop rounded out the facility's fire prevention and suppression tools. At 9:00 p.m. on February 16, 1906, fire threatened to destroy the Works in its entirety; a small electrical fire in the pattern shop spread, eventually consuming the entire structure, but was thankfully extinguished thanks to the efforts of both ALCO employees and the city fire department, resulting in the loss of only the pattern shop, which was subsequently rebuilt.[274] In addition to fire, vandalism and theft were threats to the Works, with iron, brass, and other metals presenting enticing targets for thieves. As opposed to the two watchmen who patrolled the grounds shortly after the building was constructed by Tanner and Delaney, by 1905, three night and day watchmen were present, with 29 watch stations throughout the property. Perhaps in an attempt to keep company offices and records safe from similar fires in adjacent shops, in 1909, at a cost of $32,000, ALCO built a new two-story administrative office along Hospital Street, separate from the rest of the facility, in the southeastern corner of the complex.[275]

As of 1906, ALCO Richmond was by far one of the largest employers in the Richmond area and its surrounding environs, with a workforce of approximately 2,600 earning a combined payroll of around $1.8 million.[276] Between June 1906 and February 1907, the Works delivered its single largest order ever: 75 100-ton 4-8-0 locomotives for use on the Norfolk & Western Railway. With a large workforce and enhanced shops, ALCO Richmond

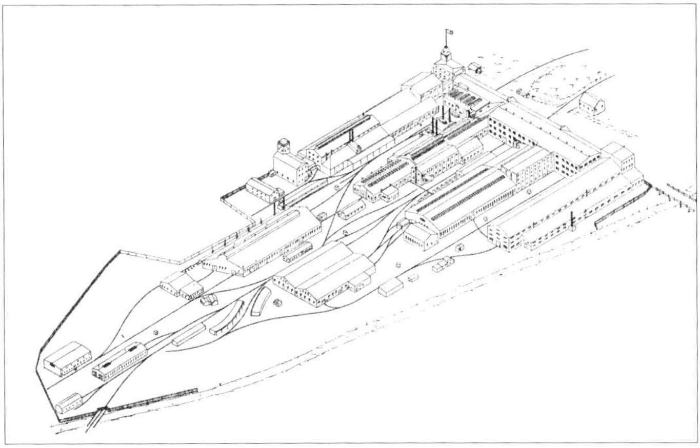

Map of ALCO Richmond, circa 1902. *John H. White Jr. Railroad Reference Collection, Archives Center, National Museum of American History, Smithsonian Institution.*

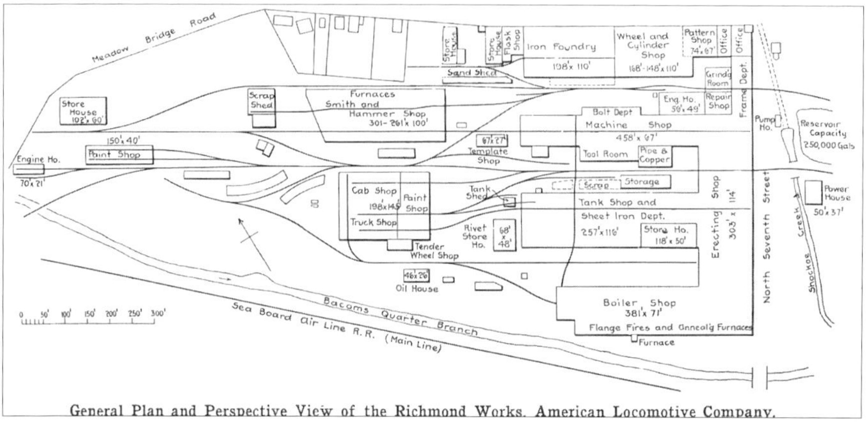

Map of ALCO Richmond, circa 1902. *John H. White Jr. Railroad Reference Collection, Archives Center, National Museum of American History, Smithsonian Institution.*

Southern Railway No. 569, 1906, 2-8-0, photograph taken at Clifton Forge, Virginia, in 1912. Pictured is conductor L.C. Schweickert *(right)*. *Nathan Vernon Madison.*

experimented with some diversification into other products. In March 1907, a 125-foot-long steel dredging ship was launched from the Newport News shipyards and then towed to Richmond the following month for installation of its ALCO-built engines, before being sent to South America to aid in the construction of the Panama Canal. In October 1908, 25 railroad cars were required to haul components, including the engines, of a massive dredge constructed at the Richmond Branch to New York and capable of moving over seven yards of earth in one scoop. The machinery was first shipped to the Suez Canal, disassembled, and then ferried to Khartoum, where the massive 500-ton dredge was reconstructed (under the guidance of an ALCO Richmond supervisor) and then towed some 800 miles farther for its intended purpose of dredging the Nile River.[277] Steam shovels were also a fairly recent addition to the ALCO Richmond catalogue, with one 70-ton specimen placed on exhibition at the Jamestown Exposition of 1907.[278]

Panics, Losses, and Corporatizing

Good times must end, and the failure of several major New York trust companies and the resultant Panic of 1907 dealt a significant blow to many throughout the capital goods sector, ALCO Richmond no exception, with new orders for locomotives dropping precipitously. The loss of work on engines invariably leads to the loss of workmen, and layoffs were frequent in such lean times. In early February 1908, 250 workmen in ALCO Richmond's blacksmith and machining departments were laid off.[279] Orders would usually pick up after such a dearth, but a constant "work-on/work-off" atmosphere, an unfortunate, but innate, symptom of the feast-or-famine model, soon became commonplace at the Richmond Branch.

If workmen were not being let go, albeit even temporarily, several longtime experienced supervisors and managers were either being siphoned off to the home office in New York or leaving the company entirely—certainly a boon for them personally but somewhat detrimental to the Richmond Branch's reserves of institutional knowledge. In 1902, Columbus K. Lassiter was appointed chief clerk to the plant manager at Schenectady, and in 1907, he was transferred yet again to the main business office in New York City, assuming the position of mechanical superintendent over all ALCO facilities. All the while, he maintained offices and residences in New York as well as Richmond, frequently commuting between the two. In July 1906, H.A. Gillis, who by that point had served nearly a decade

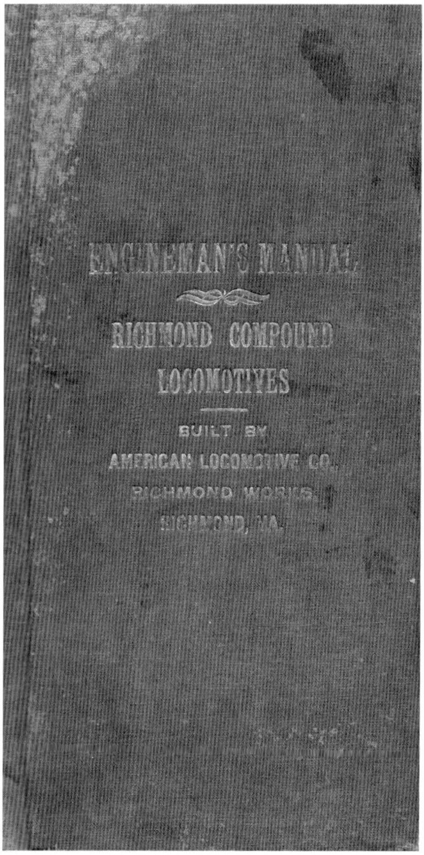

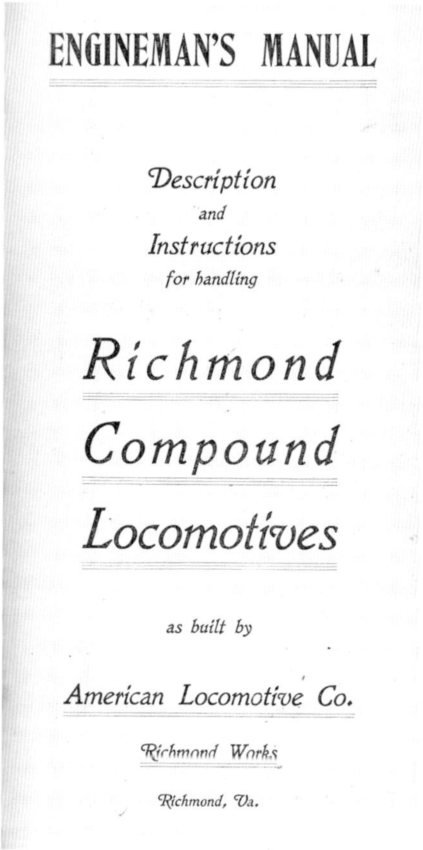

Left: Engineman's Manual—Richmond Compound Locomotives, circa 1905. *Nathan Vernon Madison.*

Right: Engineman's Manual—Richmond Compound Locomotives, circa 1905. *Nathan Vernon Madison.*

as superintendent at the Works, resigned and relocated to Pennsylvania, where he began work as manager of the Autocar Company. Autocar had begun life in 1897 producing one-cylinder three-wheeled automobiles as the Pittsburgh Motor Vehicle Company before reorganizing as Autocar three years later and relocating from Pittsburgh to Ardmore; Autocar undoubtedly benefited greatly, as Gillis was "regarded in railway circles as the ablest shop manager in the field," who carried the best qualities of both the "working machinist and the scientific mechanical engineer."[280] On May 6, 1908, a farewell party was held in honor of George E. Dubert, a ten-year veteran of ALCO Richmond and the branch's chief draftsman, who was relocating

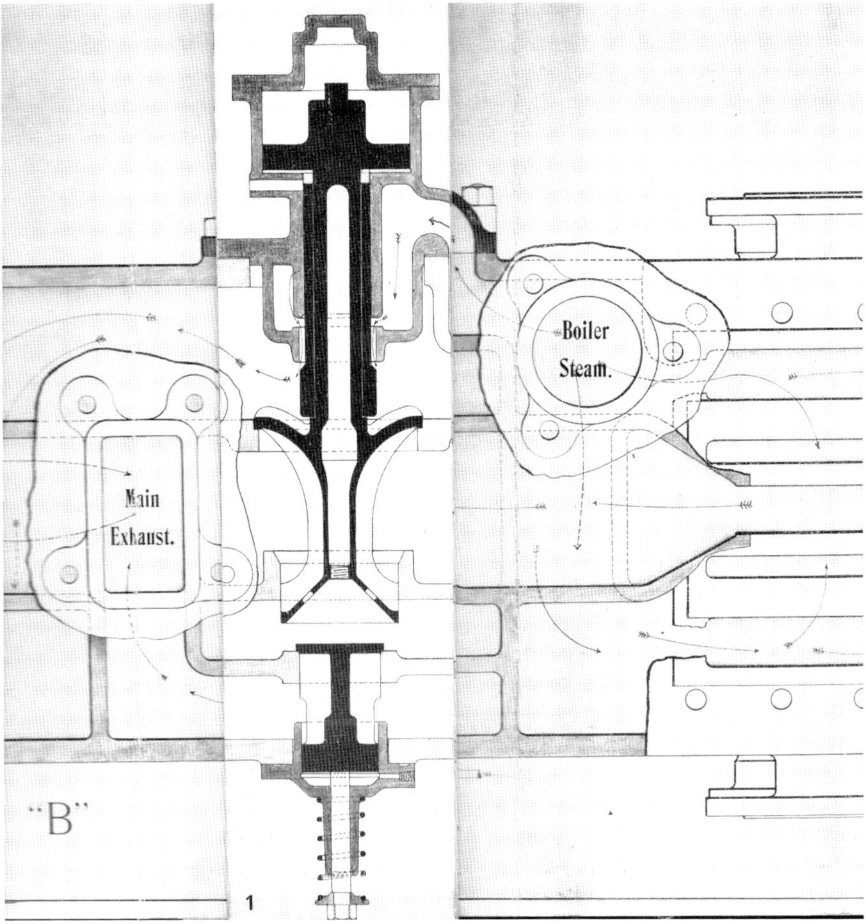

Engineman's Manual—Richmond Compound Locomotives, circa 1905. *Nathan Vernon Madison.*

to New York to take the same position at the Schenectady plant, with his direct subordinate, Thomas Carmody, assuming his place in Richmond. On the occasion of Dubert's departure, a director of the firm was quoted as stating "that it was becoming a well-known fact that whenever the company wanted a real valuable and efficient head of a department in some of the other works, the man was always found in the Richmond works."[281] While it may have been something of an embellishment to assert that every new department head or promotion from within the company *always* originated at Richmond, it was common enough to continuously diminish the amount of long-term "Richmond men" at the Works.

On November 14, 1908, Joseph Bryan awoke with severe chest pains; several days later, on November 20, he died at the age of 63 of heart failure, possibly, according to his son, the result of his having contracted typhoid fever some years earlier while supervising and assisting in the construction of a new sewer at the Works. A committee of ALCO Richmond employees, including A.O. Osterbind, telegraph operator and only the latest generation of Richmond's famed Osterbind ironworking family, penned a remembrance of Bryan to be published in city newspapers on November 24:

> *Mr. Joseph Bryan, our esteemed and much beloved friend, has gone to his reward. As employes of the Richmond Branch of the American Locomotive Company, we knew him as a broadminded, kind, generous and charitable employer. While he was at all times a busy man, yet we never found him too much engrossed in his affairs to listen to the individual cry of his men when they were in distress and needed his help and advice....Through his wise leadership and business sagacity we were offered the way and means to maintain our support, and none ever had kinder, gentler and more generous employer than Joseph Bryan.*[282]

Following Bryan's death, ALCO President Waldo H. Marshall and Vice-President Herman F. Ball traveled to Richmond, visiting Governor Claude A. Swanson alongside one of Bryan's sons, John Stewart Bryan, before touring the Richmond Branch to assess its needs in a period of transition.[283] Bryan's passing marked the definite conclusion of ALCO Richmond's control on the part of Richmond's "leading citizens" of the day; names such as Bryan and Trigg that held local sway were replaced by those from outside the city, and state, who owed more of an allegiance to ALCO, the company, as opposed to the Richmond Works, the institution. Bryan was succeeded as manager of ALCO Richmond by J.R. Marshall, previously the superintendent of ALCO's Brooks facility in Dunkirk, before being transferred to Richmond to serve under Bryan six months prior to the latter's death.[284] Marshall served only briefly in this role, as by the fall of 1911, he had been supplanted at the Richmond plant by George Gurry.

If there was anyone who could be called an "ALCO man," an employee for whom nearly their entire professional life involved the company and its subsidiaries, Gurry was certainly such an individual. Gurry, born on February 17, 1865, in London, England, immigrated to Providence, Rhode Island, with his parents, John and Martha Lewis Gurry, while still an infant.[285] Earning a degree from Brown University in mechanical engineering, he began his career at the Rhode Island Locomotive Works as a draftsman, a position he left for a brief time to assume the same role at the Brooks Locomotive Works in 1899 before returning to Providence, where he was appointed superintendent. Gurry soon relocated yet again to another ALCO facility, this time to the Longue Point plant of the Montreal Locomotive Works in 1904, shortly after its absorption into ALCO, once again as superintendent.[286] No later than November 1911, Gurry replaced J.R. Marshall as manager of ALCO Richmond following the latter's resignation to serve as manager of the Albany Foundry Company and Troy Machinery Works. Gurry was accompanied to Richmond by Walter S. Seamans Jr., another ALCO man. Seamans, who earned a bachelor's degree from Brown University as well, immediately entered into the railroading business after graduating in 1902, first with the New York, New Haven & Hartford Railroad before leaving to work in the purchasing division of the ALCO Providence facility in May 1903, followed by a stint at the Montreal Branch. Seamans transferred to the main Schenectady Works to serve as assistant manager in November 1908 and then went to the New York business office as assistant to the vice-president.[287] By the time he arrived in Richmond to serve as assistant plant manager under Gurry, Seamans was undeniably knowledgeable in the "ALCO way" of shop administration.

ALCO narrow-gauge locomotive, ALCO No. 44527, manufactured at ALCO Pittsburgh for use at the Tredegar Iron Works, 1910, 0-4-0T. *Nathan Vernon Madison. Production information courtesy of Donald R. Hensley, and Taplines (www.taplines.net).*

Gurry made efforts to maintain the relatively amicable relations his predecessors had held with both workers and the general Richmond community by continuing the annual workers beach excursions (which he would drive to himself in his ALCO automobile) and by becoming a member of the Richmond Railroad Club, serving several terms as a vice-president of the group.[288] Gurry was an enthusiastic booster for the Richmond Works and was among several officials who undertook numerous sojourns across the country to sing the company's praises—at times quite literally. During a boosting tour of the southern states in September 1912, Gurry fell ill and was unable to travel, but his place was assumed by another company official, one R.M. Strader, "a big strapping fellow, a native of Richmond and an enthusiastic 200-pound Booster." Strader, in assuming Gurry's place, joined what was known as the "Booster Quartet," a cadre of vocalists who, at each stop along their route, crooned about Richmond's preeminence.[289] The presence of Gurry and Seamans was a sign of further corporatizing at the Works, bringing it more in line with other large companies of the day. Whereas Joseph Bryan believed the Locomotive Works to be one of many means through which southern fortunes, and pride, could be reestablished, Gurry and Seamans held no such regional concerns. Relying on formal education in engineering and management, they were members of the ever-expanding managerial class that was redefining much of American business, supplanting those such as Bryan, who had largely come to their positions through a combination of family wealth, local prominence, and societal connections.

Foreign Markets

During economic distress at home, foreign orders could be relied on to alleviate some strains caused by a dearth of domestic work.[290] American locomotives enjoyed high demand across the globe in the late nineteenth and early twentieth centuries, as both Europe and developing nations in Asia sought to expand their railway networks. On average, American engines could be produced far cheaper (as much as 19 percent less, in some cases) and be delivered with greater rapidity than those from Britain, the leading locomotive exporter prior to the United States' ascension to that position in the early 1870s. In addition to cost and quick turnarounds, American locomotives were preferred for the same versatility that set them apart from those manufactured in Britain as early as the 1830s. Most of the railways in development at the turn of the century, like those in America beforehand, lacked the largely leveled paths of Britain's rail network and required an engine that could maneuver and overcome twists, turns, and rugged terrain, qualities American engines excelled at.[291]

The Richmond Works had made a name for itself as an exporter as early as 1898 with the completion of Order Nos. 2749–2765 on behalf of the State Railway of Finland. The order called for 17 ten-wheeled (2-6-0, or Mogul type) engines employing Westinghouse-brand air brakes and featuring cabs composed entirely of steel, the entire product built to metric standards; in 1900, Finland received ten additional locomotives and another ten the following year (Order Nos. 2989–2998, 3146–3157), all 4-6-0s, courtesy of ALCO Richmond.[292] At least one of these contracts was brokered in part by Jonathan Bryan, Joseph Bryan's 23-year-old son, who remained in Finland for some time, overseeing the locomotives' reassembling.[293] Of the 1900 order, one engine in particular, No. 2991 (designated No. 293 in the Finnish rail system), would achieve a notable, if infamous, place in world history. In August 1917, Vladimir Illyich Ulyanov, better known as Lenin, fled to Finland aboard No. 293 from Petrograd's (formerly Saint Petersburg) Finland Station following his return from exile and failed attempts to rouse revolution against the newly established provisional government.[294] That following October, Lenin returned to Russia aboard No. 293 once again and, in the months and years to come, ushered in a despotic regime that remains a stain on human history. The locomotive remained in the Soviet Union until 1925, when it returned to Finnish use, seeing regular service between Helsinki and Moscow until the 1950s.[295] In the intervening years, the Soviet government had bestowed a reverence on the locomotive usually reserved for saintly relics, and in June 1957, the government of Finland presented No. 293 as a gift to First Secretary of the Communist Party Nikita Khrushchev and Soviet Premier Nikolai Bulganin for placement in a museum in Leningrad (as Saint Petersburg was known from 1924 to 1991). No. 293 remains on display at Saint Petersburg's Finland Station to this day.[296]

In 1898, the Richmond Locomotive Works shipped 20 locomotives, divided between two orders of 10 4-6-0 locomotives and 10 0-6-0T locomotives, for use on Sweden's state-operated railways; the *T* in the notation signifies an engine with side tanks, cube-shaped extensions on both sides of the boiler, which increased the boiler's capacity. The reason Richmond was chosen lay in its turnaround time; the Richmond Works was capable of building and delivering all 20 engines to Sweden within seven months, whereas all of the major British firms stated they would require between 15 and 18 months.[297] This advantage continued well into the ALCO years, with a significant number of Richmond engines ordered on behalf of the ascendent Japanese Empire. Following the Meiji Restoration in 1868, which brought an end to the various shogunates that had controlled the nation for over 680 years and instituted the renewal of imperial rule under the Emperor Meiji, Japan witnessed a period of rapid industrial growth that took much of the world by surprise, railway development among many advancements. Throughout the entirety of the Meiji period (1868–1912) nearly all engines in use along Japan's railroads were foreign-made, either American, German or British in origin. Between 1873 and 1897, Japan ordered 256 engines from the United States, as opposed to 244 from Britain; between 1903 and 1907, that discrepancy had risen to 384 to 282, in America's favor.[298] ALCO had an "inside man" in the form of one Willard C. Tyler, an envoy from the Schenectady Locomotive Works (and later, ALCO) who traveled throughout Japan in the late 1890s, promoting the company's wares and securing lasting relationships with many Japanese officials, including Matsumoto Soichi, overseer of the Imperial Government Railways.[299] Tyler was not alone, as ALCO's archrival Baldwin also had set its sights on the Japanese market and provided many engines for the Empire. Most noteworthy of these was a 2-8-2 compound ordered by Japan in 1897, the first of its kind, with all succeeding locomotives based on its design referred to as a Mikado type, in reference to the title then commonly attributed to the emperor in Western nations.[300]

A commemorative pin of Finland Railways No. 293, manufactured in the Soviet Union, date unknown. *Nathan Vernon Madison.*

Tyler's efforts were not in vain, however, as engine orders began to arrive at ALCO headquarters, with many sent further down the line to Richmond; between August 1907 and March 1908, ALCO Richmond shipped a total of 129 locomotives (69 2-4-0Ts; 35 2-6-2s; 7 4-6-2s, also called Pacific types; and 18 4-6-0s) to the South Manchuria Railway, formerly the Chinese Eastern Railway, constructed by the Russian government and ceded to Japan following the latter's triumph in the Russo-Japanese War. Further, in December 1911, 12 4-6-2s arrived in Japan for use on the Imperial Government Railways, which by that year traversed nearly 5,000 miles across the home islands. By the beginning of the Taisho period (1912–1926), Japan had largely become self-sufficient in the production of locomotives. Ironically, locomotive builders' enthusiasm for the Japanese market, which included offering the latest in technological advances, aided significantly the pace at which Japan no longer needed to import engines but could instead manufacture its own.[301] It is noteworthy that it was an ALCO-built engine that pulled the Emperor Meiji's funeral train from Tokyo to his final resting place in Kyoto following his death on July 30, 1912.[302] ALCO Richmond itself was not without its own envoy to foreign countries. Upon his death on January 8, 1917, Thomas Wyatt Gentry, traveling sales agent for first the Richmond Locomotive Works beginning in 1893 and then later ALCO Richmond until his passing, was granted a column dedicated to his life and achievements in the *News Leader* the following day; his travels on behalf of Richmond and ALCO included excursions across the United States, as well as "Canada…Mexico, Cuba, San[to] Domingo, Porto [*sic*] Rico, the Hawaian [*sic*] Islands, Australia, Tasmania, New Zealand…South Africa… England and Scotland."[303]

Renewed Labor Woes

In the fall of 1911, labor unrest swelled on railroads across the country, partly due to reductions in wages throughout the industry; following a strike among boilermakers employed by the New York Central Railroad, many plants under the ALCO banner, including the main facility in Schenectady, witnessed sympathy walkouts within their own boiler shops. Despite newspapers arguing that no such strike was expected at ALCO Richmond, as no New York Central orders were being fulfilled in Virginia, on November 9, 200 boilermakers at the Richmond Works did indeed stage a sympathy strike on behalf of their brethren at ALCO Schenectady. By the workmen's own initial admissions, their reasons for striking were not personal but rather obligations born of union solidarity. In response, ALCO Richmond stated that it expected the walkout would be brief and that the men's jobs would be kept for them, when they returned—however, the boilermakers' union would no longer be recognized by the plant. "There is nothing for us to arbitrate," a company spokesman reported to the *Richmond News Leader* that day. "The men admit they have no grounds for complaint. It's just a question of common sense, and I believe the men will be wise enough to come back to work."[304]

> *But we are through with the Boilermakers' Union. Its officers admit we have lived up to our agreement with them to the last letter. They, on the other hand, have broken their agreement with us. Hereafter, so far as we are concerned, the Boilermakers' Union ceases to exist. We will enter no more agreement with them, and our boiler shops will be "open."…If necessary, we'll house and feed them. The company positively refuses to allow the union to dictate what sort of work it shall do.… We want our men back but they must be reasonable.*[305]

The company's refusal to engage with the union was not actually its call to make alone, as such decisions and negotiations would be decided not by Richmond but rather by the ALCO senior management in New York. The ensuing days contained reports of several workmen returning, proving, according to the Works' understanding of the situation, that the strike had no merit and that at least some picketers had "returned to their senses." Picketing workers began to argue that it was far more than a sympathy strike and that the Works had indeed breached portions of their contract with the workmen, regardless of the company's claims otherwise. Whatever the case, apparently enough workmen had not returned to satisfy ALCO's demands: on November 14, 11 boilermakers from outside the state, under police guard, were escorted across the picket line and into the Works. The strikebreakers were unmolested, and no violence broke out at that time, although arguments outside the confines of the facility did result in several beatings and arrests in subsequent days.[306] J.R. Marshall's brief tenure as manager of the Works had left many workmen doubtful that any sort of agreement reached with current manager Gurry could be relied on—who could say if he would not be replaced just as quickly and any progress made lost? This prompted Gurry to publish a telegram from ALCO Vice-President James McNaughton in the city newspapers reiterating that both Gurry and Seamans were contracted to the Richmond plant for no less than five years and that any agreement they entered into could be relied on thereafter.[307] On November 27, a public forum was held in Richmond's Colonial Theater along the 800 block of Broad Street (currently the site of the Library of Virginia) to explain to the general public the purpose of the strikers' actions, from their perspective. Third International Vice-President of the Brotherhood of Boilermakers Thomas Nolan argued the strikers' primary grievance lay in ALCO Richmond's alleged renunciation of the workers' right to attend their national gathering in Schenectady, at which the original New York Central strike was to be the singular topic—a right that the contract between ALCO Richmond and the boilermakers clearly granted them. Nolan continued to broadcast the workers' desire to find a cordial end to this impasse, as "amity and good feeling [had] always existed in the past between the officials of the American Locomotive Company and the workingmen."[308]

The strike, and negotiations, lingered on into the following year, with several sympathetic unions and workingmen's associations organizing drives to raise funds for the striking boilermakers. On January 13, 1912, after it was acknowledged that approximately 75 percent of the original strikers in Schenectady had grown tired of the picket lines and returned to work, the strike was called off there and at all affected plants, Richmond included. ALCO Richmond welcomed any returning workmen, although not everyone who wished to resume their labors was guaranteed a place on the shop floor. "We will continue to follow the policy the American Locomotive Company has maintained in the past," Manager George Gurry explained. "All men who apply for positions will be put to work, in case there is a place for them. Of course, we will not discharge the men who came in during the labor trouble in order to make a place for them."[309] Work once again returned to a steady pace, with 204 engines shipped out from the Richmond plant in 1912 and 225 in 1913; a temporary increase in workmen was actually required to fulfil incoming orders, with Assistant Manager Seamans making an appeal in city papers for more skilled workers, stating that "the present force of employes of the local plant is insufficient to cope with the work so as it is completed on time," even with night and day shifts.[310]

Problems at Home

As early as 1910, it had become apparent that ALCO Richmond was not receiving as many regular orders from the home office in New York as it had in years past. Not to say production ceased, as work was still ongoing, as demonstrated by the growth in output following the end of the 1911 strike. Rather, the amount of work sent Richmond's way by the New York offices could not justify a workforce of 2,500, or even 1,000, on a continuous basis; a yearly output of 225 in 1913 was quite low for a facility that could reasonably boast of a production capacity of up to 400 locomotives per annum. The 1911 strike, in addition to the workmen's stated grievances, was likely also fueled by concerns regarding job security at the Richmond Branch, as the company had begun a regular practice of hiring, or laying off, as many workers as needed relative to the number of locomotive orders to be fulfilled. Less than a year before the strike, ALCO Richmond found it necessary to temporarily lay off the entire workforce. On August 23, 1910, ALCO Richmond Manager J.R. Marshall released a statement informing all employees that the facility would be shuttered due to a "lack of material with which to work and scarcity of orders."[311]

> *We regret that the lack of work necessitates the closing of the shops for a period of about two weeks. With the completion of order R-184, we are out of new work, with the exception of orders for thirty-four engines from four different roads which we have this day received. These were taken at an exceptionally low price to enable us to hold our organization together and also in hope that there will be a resumption of business in the near future.*

This closure—estimated to result in only a fraction of the workforce returning to commence manufacture of the newly arrived orders—was but only one of several factors threatening the prosperity and very existence of the Richmond Works. And while work did continue, such "dry periods" of work would become more and more frequent as the decade progressed.

What was the cause of such slowdowns? The central reasons will be addressed in greater detail shortly, but for now it suffices to say that Richmond

Southern Railway No. 1333, 1912, 4-6-2. *Nathan Vernon Madison.*

was losing favor among the officers at the home office in New York, who, over the preceding years, had shifted an increasing amount of operations to the primary factory in Schenectady as a means of consolidating operations. Concurrently, ALCO was also beginning to diversify into other lines, such as automobiles and diesel engines, neither of which could be produced at Richmond due to workforce and infrastructure limitations. The amount of work available at ALCO Richmond, on a dependable, year-round basis, was falling more and more into question, something that was evident to management and labor alike; in May 1911, a few months before the strike, E.C. Davison, a correspondent for the International Association of Machinists' *Monthly Journal*, wrote regarding Virginia's capital that "conditions of trade in this burg are not very good at present and I would not advise our brothers to come this way with an expectation of securing work."[312]

Orders fulfilled in Richmond continued to dwindle until they came to an abrupt halt. In November 1914, following the shipping out of ten 4-8-2, or Mountain type, locomotives to the Seaboard Air Line, locomotive production ceased entirely at the Richmond Branch, affecting the livelihoods of thousands; from January through November, only 98 locomotives shipped out from the Works that year. The works at Dunkirk, Paterson (Cooke), Pittsburgh, and the main plant at Schenectady were the only ALCO shops still producing steam locomotives.[313]

Southern Railway No. 1353, 1914, 4-6-2. *Nathan Vernon Madison.*

The massive factory in the Shockoe Valley remained closed for nine months, until a new opportunity presented itself, thanks to the rumblings of war in Europe and the efforts of ALCO Richmond veteran Columbus K. Lassiter. As a direct result of both, ALCO acquired a second plant in Richmond, one with a rather winding history and often confusing string of defunct companies all its own.

5

THE BOULEVARD EXPANSION AND WORLD WAR I

1869–1917

In 1869, the Richmond Iron Works (RIW) was established at the intersection of 9th and Canal Streets, founded by Joseph Hall and chief mechanic George J. Hooper Sr. (formerly of Sampson & Pae).[314] The RIW was able to make good use of a rather cramped facility containing a foundry with two core ovens and one cupola furnace, a moulding shop, a machine shop, and a pattern storage in the attic. The RIW (alternatively known as Jos. Hall & Co.) operated for over two decades, producing everything from manhole covers and millstones to small stationary engines, until its dissolution on April 30, 1892.[315] Its assets were purchased by James Hamilton Scott and John Chamblin, employees of the firm since its inception. Scott and Chamblin, as of June 1, were joined by a new partner who brought a wealth of mechanical engineering experience to the endeavor—Alexander Delaney, formerly of the Tredegar Iron Works and the Tanner & Delaney Engine Company.[316] Delaney's presence undoubtedly brought name recognition and stability to a newly established concern, as made clear in his announcement of the partnership:

> *Having associated myself with Messrs. Chamblin & Scott in the Foundry and Machin[e] business, I hope that my long experience and familiarity with the various branches of the iron business will assure to the new company a continuance of the patronage accorded to me in the past years by my friends throughout the South during my connection with the Tanner & Delaney Engine Company, and later with the Richmond Locomotive Works.*[317]

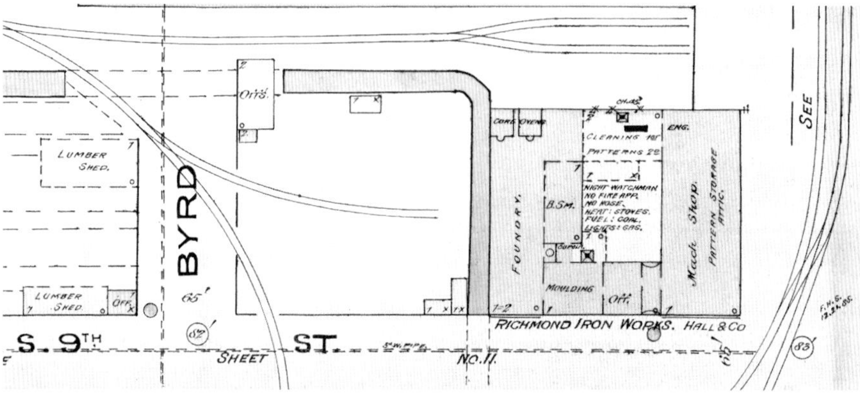

Richmond Iron Works, 1886. Sanborn Insurance Maps. *Library of Congress, Geography and Map Division, Sanborn Maps Collection.*

The connections to Tanner & Delaney went beyond the presence of Delaney himself, as advertisements for the firm proudly proclaimed, "We control the patterns of Joseph Hall & Co., and Tanner & Delaney Engine Company, and are prepared to duplicate all work formerly furnished by them."[318] The new venture did not enjoy auspicious days initially, as a fire struck the facility on December 14, setting alight the roof of the blacksmith shop and destroying a number of patterns, mouldings, and other implements, totaling a loss of around $500, a sizable sum at the time.[319] Luckily, fortunes soon rose, and stationary engines, railroad implements, and other products flowed from the facility; the RIW also gained renown for the quality of its structural iron beginning in September 1894 with Scott's successful bid, over the offers of a dozen competitors, to supply iron used in the construction of a new lighthouse along the Chesapeake Bay.[320]

In 1892, the RIW relocated to a 1.5-acre parcel at the corner of Broad Street and 15th, just downhill and east of Capitol Square, bordering Lumpkins Alley and built on the remains of what was once the infamous Lumpkin's Slave Jail; Hall had inspected several possible choices in nearby Manchester but eventually decided to remain in Richmond.[321] The need for additional space was one consideration, but far more pressing were the demands of the Richmond & Petersburg Railroad, which had long eyed the Canal Street property as a means by which to augment its presence in the city, finally purchasing it for $40,000 in February 1892.[322]

A majority of the new site consisted of its machine shop, within which were housed a blacksmith shop and tool room; adjacent to the machine shop

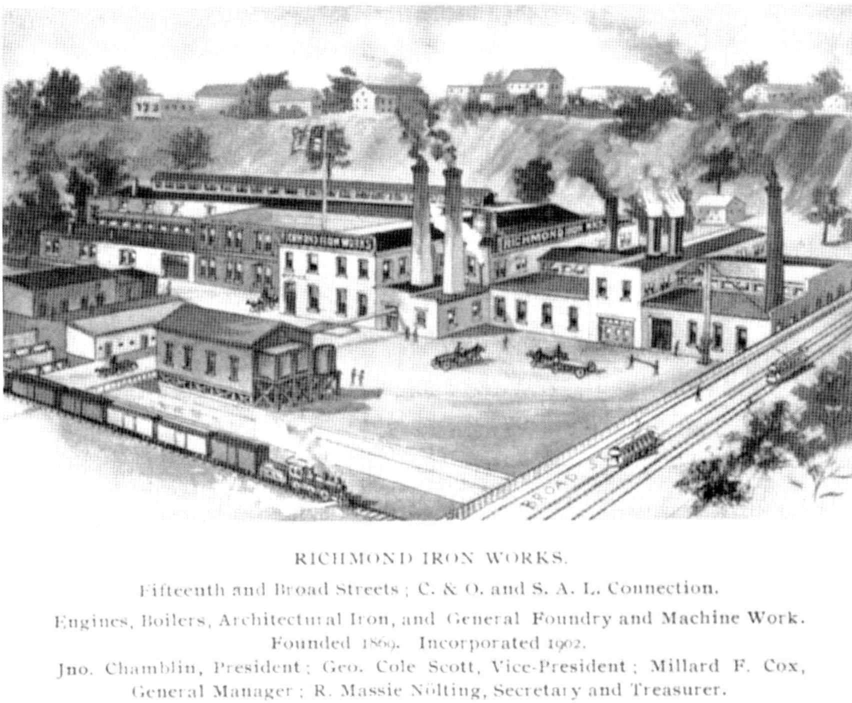

Richmond Iron Works, 1903. *From* Richmond Virginia: The City on the James, *1903.*

were the company offices and a pattern shop, as well as a pattern storage. To the north of the machine shop, between it and Broad Street, was a sizable, earthen-floored foundry that contained two cupola furnaces and a core oven. As was the case with most industrial establishments of the day, natural sunlight was used as often as possible, with kerosene lights only in the offices.[323] Scott's daughter, Mary Wingfield Scott, would often visit her father at the works, remembrances she would write about years later in her role as one of Richmond's staunchest historic preservationists.[324] In the spring of 1900, the company briefly flirted with entering the shipbuilding trade, a shipyard in Newport News having been offered to the RIW to use in the event recent bids for the construction of several government revenue-cutters proved successful; alas, success was not to be had, and the deal fell through.[325] Rumors once again swirled that May, when a group of northern investors expressed interest in constructing a shipyard in Fulton, slightly southeast of Chimborazo Hill; once again, the RIW was floated as being involved in the undertaking.[326] As with the Newport News contracts, the proposed shipyard did not materialize, and the RIW never ventured into naval projects.

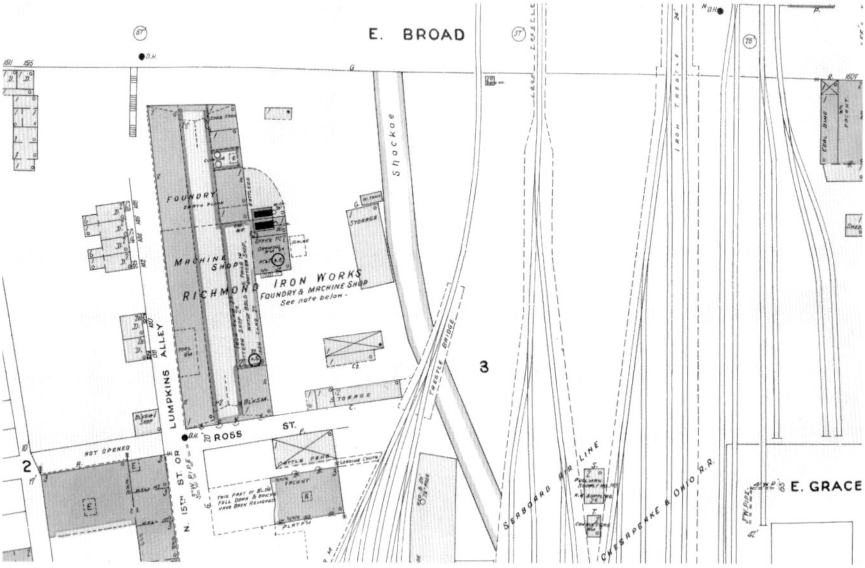

Richmond Iron Works, 1905. Sanborn Insurance Maps. *Library of Congress, Geography and Map Division, Sanborn Maps Collection.*

On May 29, 1902, the RIW was reorganized and incorporated, with a fixed capital stock of $35,000 at minimum and $100,000 maximum, with significant changes in management partly brought about by the recent death of James H. Scott.[327] Delaney had departed the firm in 1895 to assume his post with the city water department. John Chamblin retained the presidency, with Richmond financier George Cole Scott appointed vice president. Millard Fillmore Cox, who had joined the company the prior year, was named general manager/superintendent and chief draftsman. Cox, a native of Essex County born on September 3, 1866, was an "old hand" of the Richmond industrial scene, having worked at Tanner & Delaney as an apprentice draftsman from October 1881 to 1884 and the Richmond Locomotive Works from 1897 to 1901 as chief draftsman.[328] R. Massie Nolting, a 14-year veteran of the RIW, was appointed treasurer and secretary.[329] Stationary and portable engines, as well as various iron implements, accounted for the bulk of the RIW's wares, as well as structural iron. In October 1902, the RIW provided all of the iron for a $60,000 expansion of the Rosenegk Brewery along Hermitage Road, in modern-day Scott's Addition, which included three cold storages, a new bottling plant, and a new office building. In 1905, the RIW aided in the renovating and expansion of Manchester's city jail.[330]

The RIW remained at 15th and Broad until the machinations of yet another railroad, in this case the Seaboard Air Line, and its desire to incorporate the property into its freight yard, forced yet another relocation.[331] The land would eventually be sold to the railroad, and by April 1907, construction had begun on a new facility just outside (what was then) the western boundary of Richmond, in Henrico County, at the intersection of North Boulevard (modern-day Arthur Ashe Boulevard) and Leigh Streets.[332] Approximately 125 employees continued to labor at Broad Street on everything from munitions contracts for the army to structural and decorative iron and railroad accoutrements until the week of Christmas 1907, when the new facility was officially open for business. Shortly before the new location was up and running, there was a reorganization of the firm's management structures, most notably E.T.D. Myers Jr. assuming the presidency and Colonel Charles Evans Wingo and F.S. Valentine joining the board of directors.

Spread across four and a quarter acres, these expanded shops enjoyed a direct connection to the RF&P and featured a two-story office building that even included a dining hall for staff. The adjacent machine shop contained an overhead crane, 50 feet in span, that could traverse the entire length of the 100-by-100-foot building, with a secondary, smaller crane used for lighter work. Outside was a brass foundry, containing three furnaces, as well as an adjoining polishing room. North of the brass foundry and connected to the machine shop (as well as the RF&P by rail) was the foundry, of the same dimensions as the machine shop, and containing a matching 50-foot span, ten-ton capacity crane. The foundry possessed several core ovens, as well as a cupola furnace that was reportedly capable of producing around 20,000 pounds of molten iron per hour. East of these buildings and bordering the edge of the property was a blacksmith and forge shop, as well as a pattern storage, 40 by 60 feet, which continued to house, among other items, patterns sourced directly from the late Tanner & Delaney Company and likely used in repairs to engines originally produced by that company.[333] The new RIW operated its own internal fire department, with a reservoir nearby from which water could be drawn. The plant utilized both direct and alternating currents, with the former used for interior illumination and crane operation and the latter for machining. With a new facility and expanded resources, it was hoped business would expand accordingly, optimisms buoyed by a 1908, $20,000 War Department contract for 18-pound projectiles, the RIW's portion of a total $100,000 award it shared with Tredegar.[334]

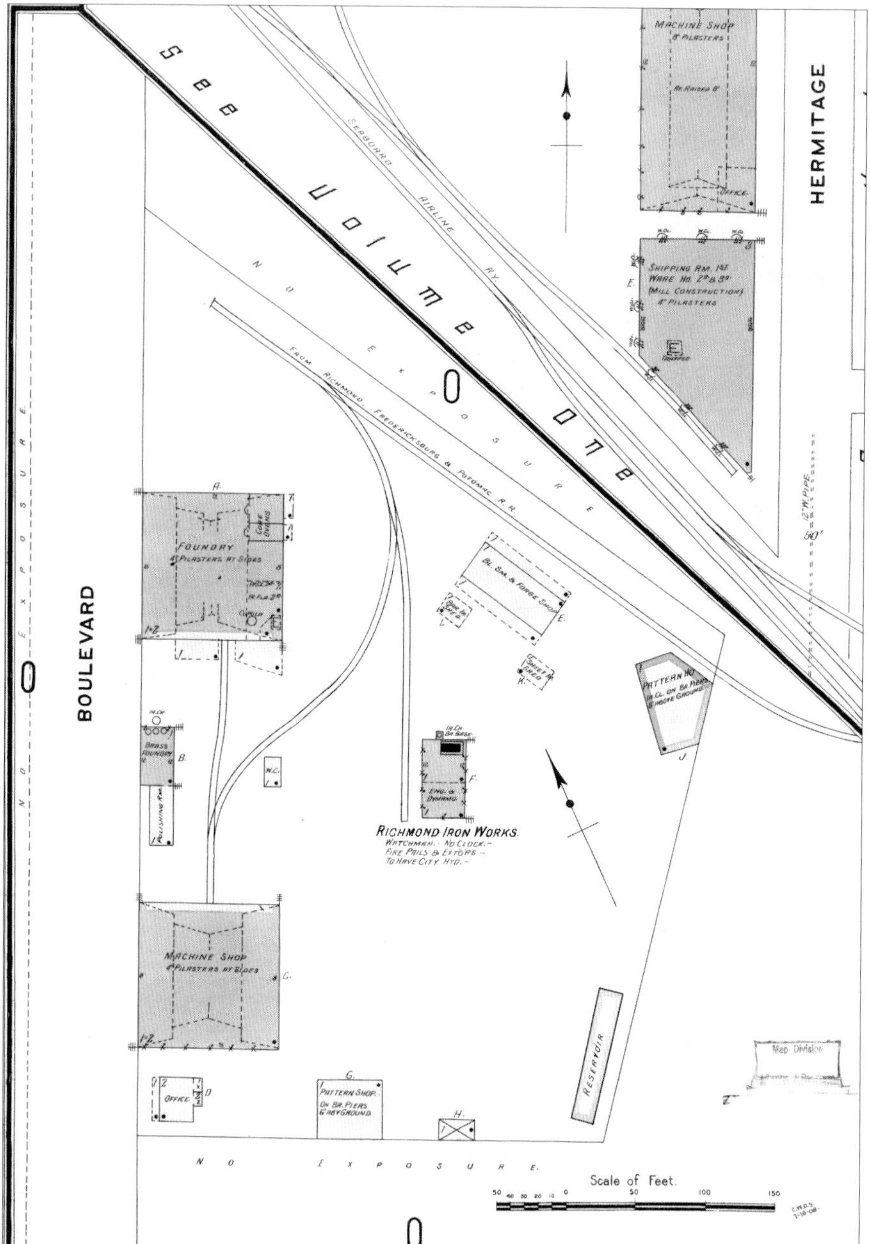

Above: Richmond Iron Works, 1908. Sanborn Insurance Maps. *Library of Congress, Geography and Map Division, Sanborn Maps Collection.*

Opposite: Charles Wingo. *From* Richmond Virginia: The City on the James, *1903.*

The first indications of trouble for the RIW may have been the departure of general manager/superintendent and chief draftsman Millard Fillmore Cox in 1908, when he resigned the firm to return to ALCO; in 1911, he would be appointed chief engineer for the Louisville & Nashville Railroad, where he designed several locomotives for that line.[335] In December 1909, the RIW ceased operations, a victim of factors beyond its abilities to overcome. Foremost, by the company's own admission, was the detrimental effects of the world's most recent financial scare. "Soon after we got possession of the plant," recounted Charles Wingo, having assumed the presidency following Myers's brief tenure, "the panic of 1907 came on, and we never recovered from that handicap."[336]

Three months later, on April 1, 1910, the Richmond Iron Works property and assets were purchased, at a cost of $75,000, by the Lancaster Automatic Railway Crossing Company, based in nearby Petersburg; Lancaster's president, M.A. Finn, intended to restart the iron works to produce railway derailment prevention devices for which he held patents, in addition to other products. The two businesses were soon combined with Finn remaining as president, and the amalgamated entity, christened the Richmond Iron Works Corporation, was formed with a maximum capital stock of $500,000 and was already accepting orders as of May 1. The sole holdover from its predecessor was R. Massie Nolting as assistant secretary and treasurer, with H.A. McCurdy, M.J. Francis, and W.H. Woody as vice-president, treasurer, and general manager, respectively.[337]

The production of railway accessories, apparently, was not Finn's sole reasoning for expanding onto the Boulevard, as on July 3, the *Times-Dispatch* reported, "It is yet a secret, but nevertheless a fact, that the company not only purposes to manufacture the goods heretofore marketed by the two companies that have become one, but in addition they will become automobile manufacturers."[338] This "secret" rapidly became the talk of the town throughout the city's and even other states' newspapers, as the automobile had only recently entered the realm of both mass production, and, more importantly, affordability for vast swathes of the American population. Horseless carriages and other forms of "locomobiles" had been attempted and produced for several decades, but it had only been a little over two years since the Ford Motor Company's introduction of the Model T in the fall of 1908. Its relatively low price and assembly line manufacture had a revolutionizing influence on the automobile industry. Numerous motor car companies had sprung up since the turn of the century—the Olds Motor Works (1899), the Buick Motor Company (1903), the Ford Motor Company (1903), and the General Motors Company (1908), to name a few—and the Richmond Iron Works Corporation was eager to enter this burgeoning market. As soon as the first demonstration vehicle, named *Battleship Grey* due to its color scheme, was unveiled, city boosters and newspapermen were proselytizing the birth of a Richmond automobile industry and the resurrection of Richmond as the most important industrial hub of the South.

> *Why should not Richmond make automobiles just as good as any that ever came from the factories in Detroit or any other town? Why should not Richmond make better automobiles—better for Virginia and for Southern roads and Virginia and Southern conditions—than any factory in the West, or in the North, or anywhere else?…That is just the way the Richmond young men who are at the head of the Richmond Iron Works got to figuring a year or two ago when they saw the big demand for automobiles and at the same time were looking for new worlds to conquer in their line of business.…The automobile industry is going to be a big thing for Greater Richmond.…Old Virginia is coming right to the front, and big Richmond with its varied manufacturing interest is right at the head of the column. All Virginia will doubtless congratulate Richmond on the establishment here of an automobile factory.*[339]

In the fall of 1910, the Richmond Iron Works Corporation began promotion and full-scale production of its new line of automobiles, appropriately dubbed the Virginian, with the first consumer model evidently purchased by one Mr. Lamar of Mississippi, "a resident of that State in whose veins flows Virginia blood."[340] The company's strategy was to corner the automobile market in the region by emphasizing both quality, by seeking out workers already experienced in automobile production, and affordability, retailing the Virginian at $3,000, fully equipped, when comparable models would normally average $5,000. The enterprise held promise, owing to both the growing popularity of automobiles at the time as well as its location, its spur track linking it directly to the RF&P, facilitating the arrival of raw materials and the shipping out of finished vehicles.[341] The entire complex had not been reconfigured to produce motor cars alone, as its brass and iron

Virginian—A-50. Price $3,000, Fully Equipped

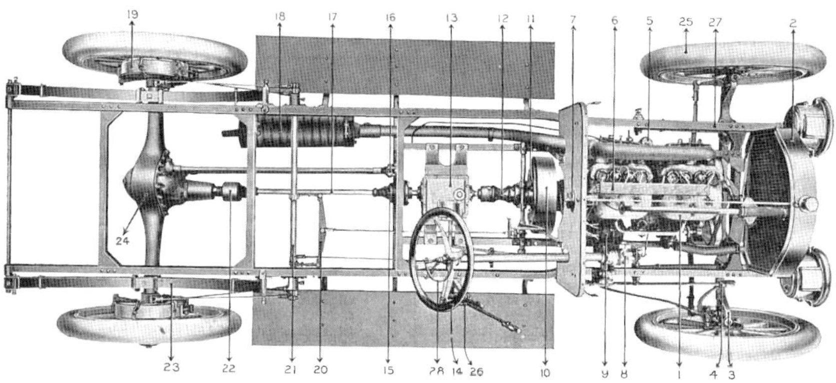

Chassis of the Virginian—A-50

Top: The Virginian Automobile, Richmond Iron Works Promotional Pamphlet, circa 1912. *Virginia Museum of History & Culture (TL160 .R5 1912).*

Bottom: The Virginian Automobile, Richmond Iron Works Promotional Pamphlet, circa 1912. *Virginia Museum of History & Culture (TL160 .R5 1912).*

foundries and machine and blacksmith shops continued to produce other items, including munitions for the navy and army. Since its construction, the plant itself had undergone several enhancements and expansions. By 1911, the blacksmith shop boasted a 3,500-pound steam hammer, and the small on-site power plant contained a 35-kilowatt Westinghouse generator for all lighting and machinery.[342] Its iron foundry was capable of a daily output of 40 tons of gray iron products, with both the foundry and machine shops now using electric cranes with a carrying capacity of at least 20 tons. The pattern shop continued to produce original designs as well as those previously used by its predecessor firms and those of Tanner & Delaney.[343]

City boosters certainly did their part in promoting the Virginian: "Known always as a city which, if called upon to do so, could furnish practically all of its necessities," wrote one reporter in November 1910, "Richmond has recently added another spoke to its wheel of commerce and industry by developing a plant which from now on will turn out high-class automobiles ranking below none manufactured either in America or in Europe."[344] Inauspiciously, however, fire swept through the factory on the evening of March 21, 1911. Beginning in the roof of the paint shop, the conflagration eventually consumed the entire building, despite the best efforts of both the plant's and the city fire departments, destroying several Virginian automobiles then under construction, a total loss amounting to $15,000.[345] Suspiciously, company ads soon appeared in city newspapers promoting the high dividends possible with, and coupons offering discounts on the purchase of, shares of the Richmond Iron Works Corporation; given the timing, this was likely an attempt to attract investors and salvage the company from a rather precarious financial footing.[346] Further unfortunate news, and admittedly bad publicity, arrived with the death of Walter Austin Miller, the foreman of the automobile department, on May 25, 1911. During a test drive outside the city limits near Yellow Tavern, in a Virginian no less, the vehicle's right rear tire was punctured and the car slammed into a tree, an impact that killed Miller instantly.[347] Even if it was later determined to be a freak accident that did not necessarily call the quality or craftsmanship of the Virginian into question, it was nonetheless a detriment to a new enterprise attempting to make its name in an already-crowded field.[348] Some investors were apparently feeling a bit uncertain about the firm's future; within weeks of the accident, classified ads in city papers were starting to appear, offering shares in the company for sale, with one day alone, July 16, 1911, quoting three separate sellers offering a total of 506 shares "for a bargain."[349]

The Virginian, despite much fanfare in the press, failed to ensure Richmond's position as the "next Detroit." As orders dwindled and workers were let go, the liquidation of the firm began in the latter months of 1911; on January 25, 1912, notices were sent to all stockholders that the firm's vice-president and secretary/treasurer had spent the several prior months "entirely liquidat[ing] your Company." With all due bills called in and remaining inventory sold, the company was left with $2,750.00 in cash on hand, which was distributed to shareholders as a final dividend; Charles

Evans Wingo, the former president of the predecessor firm, was one such investor, who received a total of $467.50 for his 85 shares of preferred stock.[350] The dispersal of any remaining assets, most notably the "entire plant of the Richmond Iron Works Corporation, consisting of lands, buildings, machinery, etc.," was placed in the hands of the bankruptcy courts in February 1912, and on May 5, 1913, its assets were sent to public auction, in hopes of salvaging the $67,000 the company still owed at the time of its dissolution.[351]

M.A. Finn, former president of the defunct automobile works, eventually purchased the now four-and-a-half-acre site, machinery included, for $53,000 in January 1914; Finn had secured a charter on October 28, 1913, for the formation of a new concern, the Henrico Iron Works, with a maximum starting capital of $25,000.[352] M.A. Finn and Stuart Johnson were named president and secretary, respectively, of the firm—a firm, however, that may have been nothing more than a holding company. No evidence survives, be it in product or any ephemera, that the Henrico Iron Works ever began operations of any sort, and slightly a year after its founding, the property once again changed hands.

And at this juncture, the plant at 1301 North Boulevard enters into the history of ALCO Richmond, although some tangential connections had existed prior; as early as 1899, the Richmond Locomotive Works carried a "Chamblin & Scott Consignment Account" in its inventory ledgers.[353] On May 9, 1915, it was announced that the American Locomotive Company had entered into agreement to lease the property for the production of munitions for Allied forces in Europe. While the United States was not involved militarily in the conflict (yet), its status as the predominant industrial force on the planet ensured that it could not remain uninvolved for much longer.

The World War and the Works

Throughout the early spring of 1915, ALCO president Waldo H. Marshall consistently and vehemently denied "wild rumors" that any sort of agreement for munitions orders had been reached with the Allied powers of Europe, even after it had been revealed that 500 lathes, specifically machined for shell manufacture, had been purchased by the company. After it was widely acknowledged that ALCO would indeed undertake munitions work, managing director of ALCO Richmond George Gurry still refused to confirm or deny that such work was to be carried on in Richmond, despite his having traveled to the Montreal Branch, where similar machinery was already in use.[354] The need for coyness or even secrecy on the company's part was to be expected, given the climate at the time. The Montreal Works, residing in what was then still a Dominion of the British Empire, could openly manufacture shrapnel for Britain and its allies. On the other hand, ALCO's plants in the United States, which was still technically (even if not in actuality, if one is being honest) a neutral country, had to tread a bit more carefully, particularly following German remonstrations regarding American firms such as Remington and DuPont fulfilling Allied orders.

The House of Morgan played a crucial role in securing munitions production at ALCO Richmond. The British government named J.P. Morgan & Co. as its designated purchasing agent in the United States in January 1915, an honor France also granted that May.[355] Shortly thereafter, Morgan worked tirelessly to aid the Allied cause in securing munitions contracts with American manufacturers. ALCO was among the first enterprises Morgan & Co. approached regarding such contracts, already inked by the British government and simply awaiting acceptance. The first agreement for munitions ALCO accepted was worth $10 million and was divided between the Dunkirk and Richmond plants; Richmond's portion called for 1.25 million loaded 18-pounder, 3.3-inch shrapnel shells (complete sans fuses) and 2.5 million 18-pounder cartridge casings (complete, but not loaded).[356] ALCO's May 20, 1915 acceptance of such a lucrative contract is not surprising; the fact that it ended up being sent to Richmond, however, is. Not only had the Richmond plant been shuttered for the previous nine months, but it was also wholly unsuited to munitions fabrication by any conceivable measure. Locomotive production is, understandably, quite different from methods employed to produce shells and shrapnel, necessitating a near-total conversion of the entire plant. Further, the former workforce had no munitions experience. If that was not enough, time restraints provided additional obstacles; within four months' time, at least 50,000 shells were to be delivered, with that number increasing incrementally until the contract's expiration date, June 20, 1916, although this was later extended by several months. A summation of the company's experiences during the war years credits one man in particular with seeing such daunting obstacles through, and if later reminiscences on the part of ALCO Richmond employees are to be believed, this was Columbus K. Lassiter, then mechanical superintendent for all of ALCO.

> *Other manufacturers were signing similar contracts and it was evident to one man, and a Richmond man, too, that there would be a serious shortage of certain machine tool specialties. He anticipated the contracts by quickly forecasting requirements and closing out with certain machine tool manufacturers for their entire output. This assured his own requirements if the contracts were closed, and if not, the contracted specialties could be sold at a profit. This is one of the secrets of the quick start made in production, which is now a matter of record.*[357]

The Works' Mechanical Department immediately set about devising procedures and preparing for needed tool orders; it was left to the Manufacturing Division to redesign the plant from the ground up and turn it into a fully functioning munitions plant. Steam hammers, furnaces, and cranes were among the roughly 730 pieces of heavy equipment that needed to be moved out if shell manufacture were to commence. Securing the $2 million worth of new machinery was a task in and of itself; with other producers in Richmond hungry for contracts as well, equipment such as lathes and presses were on a "first come, first served" basis, resulting in ALCO Richmond stationing men at select factories to ensure they were served first. This overhaul was not limited to machinery but the infrastructure of the Shockoe Valley plant itself.

> *Heavy concrete foundations had to be demolished. The power plant of necessity had to be enlarged to meet the new requirements. Additional transformer and motor generator sets had to be installed to utilize purchased power. A steam engine, driving a generator of 350 K.W. capacity, was replaced by a gas engine and producer plant having a 750 K. W. capacity.... In the meantime, the new equipment was coming in and being installed.*[358]

Nearly every department of the Works was either reconstructed or redesigned to fit its new purpose, purged of its equipment and new flooring installed; the former erecting shop was remade into one enormous machine shop, and the former boiler shop was repurposed as a forge shop, complete with hydraulic presses for shell casing manufacture. Owing to the approximately 260,000 gallons of oil used monthly, several large storage tanks were installed on-site. Delivery of machine tools, as well as raw materials, began two weeks after the contract was accepted, reaching at times over 400 full train car loads monthly, with this number decreasing slightly after all needed tools had been acquired.

The United States experienced an economic recession between January 1913 and December 1914, the aftereffects of which were still felt in May 1915, resulting in a large and responsive reservoir from which to draw workers. A majority of these potential employees, however, had little to no mechanical skills, necessitating a thorough yet hasty training curriculum. ALCO president Marshall held reservations that such a program could be devised and, more importantly, prove effective. George Gurry responded to these doubts first by traveling to and studying establishments engaged in similar work in both the United States and Canada (the aforementioned trip to the Montreal Works); Gurry then instituted a program by which men were specifically educated, by the Works' chief draftsman and shop superintendents, in one function and one function alone, drastically diminishing the time spent in training. This regimen was highly effective, resulting in munitions that were never once rejected by inspectors and allowed the Works to employ, at its height of productivity, 9,000 men.

Training is nothing, however, without resourcefulness in the face of unexpected obstacles, as demonstrated by challenges encountered when production began on the requested shrapnel shells, particularly the bullets housed therein. Successful manufacture of the bullets required a precise combination of two metals, 88 percent antimony and 12 percent lead; all initial attempts at this mixture repeatedly met with failure, the metals not alloying as needed. It was soon learned, however, that the products of a Niagara Falls battery plant used the same metals, in the same proportions. Thus, an ALCO Richmond man was immediately dispatched to secure employment at this facility and observe its operations for a fortnight, before quitting and returning to Richmond. Thanks to this firsthand experience, the process was then perfected and no further issues regarding it encountered. The bullets were then cooled, reheated, and placed into a stamping machine replete with dies that would mould them into their final form; however, the relative softness of the material resulted in a fair number of malformed bullets exiting the machine, deficiencies that risked rejection on the part of British inspectors. As 349 bullets were required in each shrapnel shell, or 436 million bullets weighing 5,320 tons in total, the cost and labor outlays conceptually required to find and remove any such defects would be astronomical. Salvation came with the invention of a 12-foot-long wooden trough with meticulously measured slots that, when placed directly under the stamping machine, separated the defective from the flawless bullets as they dropped, saving the company an immeasurable amount of time, money, and manpower.[359]

Security around the Works was understandably heightened as munitions production commenced. Threatening letters from "cranks and enemy sympathizers" were common, but no genuine threats ever materialized. Around midnight on February 3, 1917, the same day President Wilson severed all diplomatic ties with the German Empire, plant manager George Gurry was awakened by a call from a troubled employee who claimed to have overheard talk of a potential plot to dynamite the ALCO Richmond facility. Following up on Gurry's concerns, several police officers spent the night at the Works—however, no evidence of a saboteur plot was ever discovered, and the initial warning was simply ascribed to wartime paranoia.[360] Throughout the period of ALCO Richmond's role as a munitions plant, several security measures were implemented, including regular patrols along the 1st and 5th Street viaducts. One hundred armed sentries patrolled the outside parameter of the plant 24 hours a day, with massive floodlights used during the night watch.

Nature provided its own encumbrances as well, thanks to several floods that inundated Shockoe Valley. Early in 1915, while a sewer was being repaired on Bacon's Quarter Branch, a small stream that ran under the Works and flowed into Shockoe Creek, a particularly heavy rain caused the branch to overflow and flood the shops' floors, up to four feet in some areas. While most equipment was spared serious impairment, the Works' office suffered heavily—substantial volumes of internal records were destroyed, conceivably explaining the scarcity of extant company archives today.[361] A second flood occurred later that week, but the damage was largely mitigated thanks to the prodigious deployment of sandbags. Neither flood resulted in a slowdown of work.

While the ALCO Richmond plant was overhauled to facilitate shell manufacture, the newly acquired Boulevard Branch's purpose was to keep the two processes of manufacturing, and then loading, shells safely segregated. Richmond city regulations allowed only enough gunpowder within city limits, in a single space, to allow for ten hours' worth of operation; therefore, to supply the newly built powder magazine at the Boulevard site, a larger magazine was maintained from which daily deliveries were made, about four miles outside city limits at Strawberry Hill. Special precautions were taken on the part of the workmen, with all metal items removed from their person, lest an unintentional spark ignite a calamity; all workers also donned felt slippers when working at the loading site. Following completion, batches were ready for testing and shipment. Each batch, or series, of completed shrapnel and cartridge cases had two drawn for testing at the

Cape May Proving Grounds in New Jersey. Upon a successful assessment, which every series produced at ALCO Richmond achieved, the series was ready for shipment. As the United States' munitions output increased, space on merchant ships was scarce, and large orders often went unshipped for some time, necessitating the acquisition of several warehouses throughout Richmond for temporary storage; once Richmond was exhausted in that regard, storehouses in Newport News and even Baltimore were procured.

Further Calls for Munitions

While in the midst of completing this initial order, a second contract was signed in December 1915 that called for 210,000, 4.5-inch explosive shells; both were fulfilled by August 1916. These orders completed, ALCO Richmond was prepared to undergo yet another refit, in this case for a reversion back to locomotive production, with two railroad orders already having arrived. However, August 1916 brought a third munitions contract, and those plans were temporarily shelved, with the received locomotive orders redirected to other ALCO facilities. This new contract presented its own set of problems. The nature of the war had changed in the preceding year, as traditional military engagements devolved into trench warfare along the western front. Accordingly, artillery demands were modified; a dependence on shrapnel and cartridge casings diminished in favor of the high-explosive shells that soon came to define no man's land. This new $25 million contract, all of which was to be fulfilled in Richmond, called for 180,000 6-inch, 300,000 8-inch, and 125,000 9.2-inch high-explosive shells.[362] The glaring difference between this order and those prior was a matter of weight—a 9.2-inch shell, for example, weighed approximately 253 pounds, as opposed to a 4.5-inch shell's 27.5 lbs. For the most part, entirely new machinery was needed to produce these substantially heavier shells, and thus another refit was required, which lasted from August to October 1916. The Works' usable floor space was expanded by as much as 15 percent to accommodate the new presses, furnaces, and over 1,000 lathes that were ordered to fulfill the contract. New shafts and belts for machinery reached into miles in length, and new floors, to support the massive weight of the incoming machines, were installed. A three-mile-long system of conveyers carried the massive shells along the production process; 840 quarter-ton chain hoists also aided in transportation, as did nine inclined elevators across the shops.

This new contract also brought new labor woes to the forefront. Workers had their pick of job prospects, as nearly every establishment was hiring due to wartime contracts. Between August, when the first orders were complete, and October, when the plant was ready to fulfill the latest contract, most workers had already moved on, with only 15 percent of the former workforce returning. Even after employment once again reached desirable levels through various recruitment efforts, competition continued to draw workers away. Increased pay and overtime aided in retaining many workers, but not entirely, as a worker turnover rate of 25 percent on the first two contracts swelled to over 40 percent with the third.

Following America's official entry into the war, ALCO held a massive, patriotic rally at its Shockoe Valley plant on April 21, 1917. Lieutenant Governor James Taylor Ellyson gave a keynote address, quoting from President Wilson's declaration of war to Congress and extolling the virtues of the war effort to a crowd reported to be "8,000 Shop Men and 2,000 Office Men," a number augmented by visitors from other ALCO branches. Patriotic music, courtesy of an all-ALCO employee band, played as 15 American flags were hoisted above the Works, one for each department, with a 16th Red Cross flag hoisted atop the Works' infirmary.[363]

As this third contract was nearing completion, the Boulevard Branch began to assume the form most recognizable to modern visitors, with the removal of the brass foundry between the iron foundry to the north and the machine shop to the south, and the bridging of the 180-foot gap between the two to create a single, massive brick building.[364] While the initial leasing of the Boulevard property was a necessity for safely loading shells, its continued usage by ALCO would not be predicated on munitions alone. Foreign orders began to decrease as European countries finished constructing enough domestic munitions plants to meet their needs and as the presence of German U-boats made transportation across the Atlantic all the more precarious. The Richmond Branch completed its munitions work in August 1917. Many firms involved in similar efforts simply resumed the same in service of American armed forces, but this was not the case for ALCO Richmond. Now that the "Shell Game," as employees referred to the munitions work, was accomplished, a return to locomotive production finally commenced.

6

A RETURN TO LOCOMOTIVES AND THE END OF THE LINE

1917–1927

The return of locomotive production to Shockoe Valley was in many ways a complete reversal of the retooling needed for shells and shrapnel. With machinery removed, floors taken up and locomotive equipment reinstalled, the plant was fully prepared to resume locomotive orders that October. A small amount of equipment was preserved, as it could easily be repurposed; a sizable portion, however, was sold to other companies involved in munitions work, while approximately 700 tons worth of machinery and tools were simply scrapped.

Machines could be easily repurposed, but men could not, and only 5 percent of the Works' current retinue were skilled enough to be retained for locomotive work; small amounts of the "old guard" who were present before locomotive production ceased in 1914 returned, but a vast majority were gainfully employed elsewhere. The remainder of the workforce ALCO Richmond could muster were not deemed the most dependable. Many "drifters" were hired, remained for a week or two and then moved on; others, while competent workmen, were wholly unsuited for the labor required. One anecdote from those days involved a professional engineer who, inquiring about the uninspired approach a planer brought to his work, was met with the reply, "You know, pard, I've only been on the job three weeks....I'm a bartender by trade."[365] Monthly turnover hovered around 25 percent briefly but steadily decreased as more skilled hands were found, although issues with itinerant workers remained.

Acquiring needed resources remained a persistent issue just as it had with munitions, and obtaining raw materials for locomotives proved taxing, with iron, steel, machine tools, and even coal difficult to procure at times. Richmond employed a small group of men, tasked with ensuring materials arrived, as needed.

> *Nothing but persistent fighting and systemized follow-up methods kept the materials coming along. Telegraph, telephone and tracing by special messenger were daily used and any expedient possible was availed of, as different conditions arose.…Ten men were on the road continually. They followed trains through to the congested junction yards and after locating their cars, used every possible means to get them into the train made up, meanwhile keeping constantly in touch the Richmond Plant.*[366]

The cessation of foreign munitions contracts did not result in ALCO abandoning the Boulevard Branch; rather, it purchased the property outright for $75,000, assuming its $25,000 outstanding mortgage.[367] In its annual report to investors, ALCO explained its reasons for purchasing this secondary site in Richmond:

> *As part of the plan of restoring the Richmond plant, and with the purpose of obtaining an immediate increase in the foundry capacity of that plant for locomotive work, the company purchased on June 25, 1917, the land and buildings of the Henrico Iron Works Corporation at Richmond, Va., suitable, with improvements which can be quickly installed, for making locomotive gray iron castings.…It is the purpose of the management to manufacture as much of the material entering in large quantities into the construction of locomotives as can be produced by the company to economic advantage.*[368]

With the intention of returning to locomotive production, ALCO Richmond began placing ads in local newspapers for workers, both skilled and unskilled, as early as September. Early that October, when locomotive work resumed, approximately 2,000 men were employed at both sites collectively, those accustomed to locomotive building fortunately representing a growing proportion. The Richmond Branch was once again in operation and producing locomotives, though not enough to buoy any hopes that the frequent downturns in production seen before 1914 were solidly in the past.

All shell-making machinery having been dismantled and replaced with those conducive to locomotive construction, the Boulevard Branch came to be known as the Accessories Plant, or later simply as ALCO Works, producing throttle and piston valves, staybolts and other accoutrements for use on the locomotives produced at the Shockoe Valley site and other ALCO branches. In early 1918, ALCO appointed Ross Anderson, previously superintendent of the company's Pittsburgh division, as manager of the Accessories Plant.[369] Despite ceasing the Shell Game, ALCO Richmond did not falter in its support of the war effort. The Richmond Branch was among several firms in the city to establish a war savings society, promoting government war bonds purchases among its workers and their families, all in an effort, as was the common cry among these recently formed groups, to "trim the Kaiser."[370]

On April 18, 1918, John Mitchell Jr., editor of the *Richmond Planet*, was invited to speak at ALCO Richmond at the behest of a committee composed of the plant's African American workforce during a Liberty Bond drive. White and Black workmen attended the event, officiated by R.W.

The presses of John Mitchell Jr.'s *Richmond Planet*, powered by a six-horsepower stationary engine, manufactured by the Richmond Locomotive Works from Tanner & Delaney designs, circa 1899. *Nathan Vernon Madison.*

Whiting, a director of Jackson Ward's Mechanics Savings Bank; the ALCO Richmond band furnished music, and a cadre of White workmen provided Mitchell and Whiting with a walking tour of the Works.[371] Connections between Mitchell and ALCO Richmond went back several decades, as the six-horsepower stationary engine that powered the *Planet*'s presses was originally manufactured by the Richmond Locomotive Works, based on Tanner & Delaney designs, and purchased by the *Planet* from the Richmond Iron Works in the late 1890s.[372]

Bond drives and other activities continued on, nearly up until the Armistice of November 1918; that October, J.M. Fowler, foreman of ALCO Richmond's iron foundry, announced his intention to organize a "100 percent club" among the 300 workmen in his department—deemed successful only after every man had vowed to purchase at least one savings stamp.[373] In all, Liberty loan subscriptions on the part of ALCO Richmond employees over the course of the war totaled $426,700, or over $7 million in 2022.[374]

Fluctuations and Uncertainties

Talk of the Richmond Works being shut down or reduced to merely a repair shop had begun circulating as early as 1903, as noted in correspondences between Joseph Bryan and ALCO president Callaway:

> *It has been diligently spread abroad here as coming directly from Pittsburg* [sic] *that the Richmond Locomotive Works were to be shut up and moved away. This, of course, is absurd, but I would like to have your distinct authority to state that management of the American Locomotive Company has no purpose whatever of interfering with the regular operation of the Richmond Locomotive Works, and that they will receive their due proportion of all business that is to be done.*[375]

These rumors were indeed soon quashed. However, with several ALCO plant closures in ensuing years, and the termination of engine production at Richmond for most of the world war, such concerns were continually fueled, even after the postwar return to locomotive construction.

Locomotive production across the United States dropped significantly following the end of the First World War, for several reasons both international and domestic. While an ascendant Asia and continued industrialization throughout North and South America provided somewhat steady orders, the same could not be said for war-torn Europe. "We have been receiving a fair amount of business from the Far East and the Pan-American countries and believe they will continue to order," Andrew Fletcher, president of ALCO as of January 1917, wrote to investors on February 28, 1920.[376]

> *A large share of our inquiries are from European countries undergoing reconstruction because of the war and whose present financial resources are such as to necessitate deferred credit payments. In some cases the inquiries have been based on an exchange and barter basis. Until those governments and their finances have become more stabilized the business accepted from them, absorbing, as it would, considerable of our working capital, should be restricted to conservative financial risk.*[377]

The cessation of hostilities in Europe coincided with a drop in the number of steam engine sales within the United States as well, across the domestic locomotive industry, particularly among the "Big Three" of ALCO, Baldwin, and the Lima Locomotive Works of Ohio. Only 214 locomotives were ordered in 1919 from American locomotive shops, before rising sharply to 1,998 in 1920 and then back down to 239 in 1921; this was a market suffering high fluctuation due to several issues, not least of which were postwar recessions that lasted through the summer of 1921.[378]

On some level, the federal government's war measures provided some relief in such lean times. Cost vacillations, shipping delays, and workers' strikes throughout America's railroads were all too common in the early twentieth century, throughout a jumbled national rail network managed by over 400 separate companies. Such issues were not only impermissible but also considered a threat to national security following the onset of World War I and particularly after America's joining the Allies in April 1917. With military and related transport taking precedence, and acting under the powers granted by the Army Appropriations Act of 1916, President Wilson issued orders in late 1917 that effectively nationalized the nation's railroad network. In March of the following year, the United States Railroad Administration (USRA) was created, with Williams Gibbs McAdoo, formerly secretary of the treasury (and Wilson's son-in-law), chosen to helm an agency that succeeded in bringing some rationality to the industry by regulating rates, consolidating routes, and raising wages for railroad workers across the board.[379] Another improvement owed to the USRA was the issuance of standardized locomotive designs to American locomotive manufacturers. Before the administration's dissolution on March 1, 1920,

1,856 engines were built to USRA specifications, including 85 from ALCO Richmond, all delivered to the government between March and December of 1919, assuring much-needed periods of steady work at the plant.[380] These included 10 4-6-2 Pacifics for the Erie Railroad in April 1919 and 20 massive 2-8-8-2 articulated engines on behalf of the Virginian Railway between June and August 1919. The USRA gained an additional 65 2-10-0 (also known as Decapods) ALCO Richmond locomotives when it leased the entire complement of Order No. R-266, originally placed by the Russian government but rendered undeliverable due to the Bolshevik Revolution, all of which required reconfiguration to run on the United States' standard-gauge tracks.[381] After the USRA's dissolution, the return of railroads to private overview, and the subsiding of the postwar economic malaise, longtime customers began to place orders to buoy their rolling stock and to upgrade along the standards established by the USRA.

While not a single locomotive was shipped from ALCO Richmond for the entirety of 1915 through 1917, from January 1918 through December 1919, 337 locomotives shipped out from the Works, despite several labor disputes and walkouts, including a brief strike of 150 boilermakers due to the dismissal of a fellow union worker, in July 1918.[382] From 1920 through 1921, 152 locomotives were shipped—in 1922, only 91. Larger numbers were shipped in 1923 and 1924, 184 and 195, respectively, before dwindling

Southern Railway No. 4813, 1923, 2-8-2. *Nathan Vernon Madison.*

to 68 in 1925 and then more than doubling to 163 in 1926. A consistent workforce was not tenable when demand fluctuated as widely as it did between 1925 and 1926's fulfilled orders.[383] Between January and March 1926, the C&O received 50 ALCO Richmond Mikados; this was the last large order the Works received, as a majority of those going forward contained fewer locomotives each, oftentimes numbering between 5 and 10, with several shipped in 1926 and 1927 requesting only a single engine per each order. Lulls in production, and resulting layoffs, were becoming more and more common. Both internal and external factors led to the drought of orders going Richmond's way. As mentioned previously, ALCO's plans for its future did not necessarily include the Richmond Works; this was true before the war, and it was still true after—the Shell Game and the resumption of orders between 1917 and 1927 were a stay of execution, not a pardon.

The years preceding and immediately following World War I were a period of transitions, consolidations, and diversification on ALCO's part that would eventually see the firm lessen, and then outright abandon, steam locomotive production. As early as 1909, with the cessation of locomotive production at the Dickson Works in Scranton, efforts were being made to close what were considered superfluous facilities in the name of consolidating production in only select factories, Schenectady and Montreal in particular. The Rogers Works of Paterson closed in 1913; the Pittsburgh plant shuttered in 1919; and the Cooke Works, also in Paterson, closed in 1926, with its property being divided up and sold to several smaller firms in 1929.[384] In the event these shuttered facilities were kept in ALCO's possession, they largely served as storage and warehousing facilities, if used at all.

In 1906, ALCO began producing automobiles, largely at the Providence shops, following an expansion of those works for this purpose, with servicing shops established in Chicago, Philadelphia, and numerous other cities across the country. ALCO had acquired the rights to produce American versions of the French Berliet until 1908, when it dropped that license and began producing its own models; despite expenditures totaling as much as $6 million over the course of the entire venture and several cars winning a number of high-profile races, only 5,000 ALCO automobiles were produced between 1906 and 1913. Despite claims from ALCO vice-president Leigh Best in July 1913 that "we have never entertained discontinuing the manufacture of Alco motor trucks, motor cars and taxicabs," and that "[q]uite the contrary, we have started a vigorous campaign and intend to go after this business stronger than ever," the very

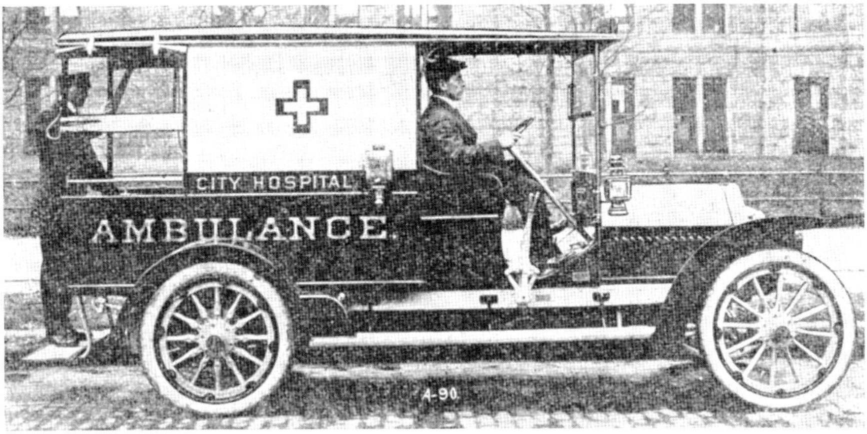

ALCO-built ambulance for Richmond, circa 1912. *Nathan Vernon Madison.*

next month ALCO president Waldo Marshall announced the company was indeed ceasing automobile production altogether, as the business had never managed to turn much of a profit.[385]

Beginning in the late 1890s, German engineer Dr. Rudolph Diesel strove to discover a method of producing motive power without the substantial loss of fuel efficiency shared by all steam-driven engines. Diesel postulated that an engine using the high temperature of air in a compressed cylinder to ignite injected fuel (as opposed to the use of spark plugs used in other engines, such as those in automobiles) could greatly elevate the ratio of thermal efficiency.[386] The process of refining the diesel engine continued for years to come; their obvious advantages over steam engines were realized and demonstrated successfully, particularly with the advent of diesel-electric engines, wherein a diesel engine powers a generator, which in turn powers electric, or traction, motors attached to the locomotive's driving wheels. As early as 1904, ALCO was tinkering with diesel engines, and in 1924, the first diesel-electric ALCO locomotive was produced for commercial use, for New Jersey's Central Railroad.[387] Aside from much higher efficiency levels, diesel locomotives required fewer hands to operate, thus lowering labor costs, and were less susceptible to explosions and other mishaps, reducing exposure to repair expenses and litigation. Diesel engines also offered a more streamlined assembly-line manufacturing process using standardized parts, as opposed to the high customization on steam engines, placing greater control in the hands of the producer rather than the customer.[388] ALCO was admittedly slow to understand the threat diesel posed to the steam locomotive market, due to both an entrenched corporate culture that valued tradition above all else, as well as the exorbitant refits required for a shift from steam to diesel engine production. When the need for such a shift was fully realized, Richmond was not an ideal site for such investment, as it lacked, when compared to other cities, a sizable workforce experienced in diesel engines. Moreover, the built-to-demand tradition of steam locomotive production, and the facilities constructed for it, would not transfer easily to the mass-production model used in diesel engine fabrication.[389]

As capital was being expended for facility upgrades, the Richmond plant itself was not a recipient of such outlays. During the lean times in the capital goods market following the Panic of 1907, ALCO invested $3.5 million in renovations and reconfigurations to several of its facilities. However, very little of what was appropriated went to Richmond, a significant portion instead used to reconfigure the Rogers Branch in Paterson to serve as ALCO's sole plant for small locomotives, as well as steam shovels and other construction machinery (such as the large dredges Richmond had produced recently), cutting other plants, particularly Richmond and Scranton, off from this product line entirely.[390] ALCO Richmond could be reconfigured for some items, such as munitions during World War I, but as far as remaining a contender in the capital goods arena, the plant's continued existence was irrevocably tied to the fortunes of the steam locomotive market.

The loss of experienced, long-term ALCO Richmond employees continued into the 1910s and 1920s; J.B. Rountree, who joined the firm in 1891 and had retained the position of foundry foreman for most of those years, resigned in August 1913 to accept a similar role at the rival Lima Locomotive Works in Ohio.[391] Walter S. Seamans Jr., who had joined ALCO Richmond as assistant manager following Joseph Bryan's death, resigned in February 1917 to become plant manager for Pennsylvania's Eddystone Munition Corporation. During his tenure, Seamans was "one of the most popular 'bosses' a Richmond industrial plant has had in recent years. He always took an active part in the plans of the men under him, and knew practically all of them by name."[392] Seaman's departure left the branch devoid of yet another experienced voice in management and affected the remaining workforce directly, as apparently a significant number of his longtime subordinates at Richmond elected to follow him to Eddystone.[393] Just as these shuffling of assets and resignations were ongoing, the Richmond Branch lost one of its staunchest supporters in the person of Columbus K. Lassiter. Lassiter, as of February 1, 1917, was appointed vice-president of manufacturing for all of ALCO.[394] Lassiter had upheld warm relations with the Richmond workmen during his rise through ALCO's management.

For several years, Lassiter served, alongside Gurry and Seamans, on the entertainment committee for the company's annual Buckroe Beach holiday, and before the war, Lassiter personally oversaw the donation and maintenance of steam pumps, stationary engines, and electric motors for use and study by students at the Virginia Mechanics' Institute, with classes taught by ALCO Richmond staff.[395] Many Richmond workmen, in later years, attested to feeling that they had a strong supporter in Lassiter, a voice for their needs who was firmly ensconced in ALCO's hierarchy. Alas, Lassiter resigned from ALCO on April 20, 1922, to become president of the Consolidated Machine Tool Corporation of America, an amalgam of smaller firms he had helped create; less than a year later, on March 3, Lassiter passed away.[396] The loss of one of Richmond's most prominent advocates within ALCO's central leadership all but ensured that it would not be shown favor as the directors worked to centralize the company's assets and plan for a future not wholly reliant on steam.

Increased diversion of work to Schenectady, as well as issues regarding poor workmanship and questionable professionalism, began to overshadow ALCO Richmond's proud heritage. Worker error in August 1919 seemingly caused an oxygen-hydrogen tank on the premises to explode, damaging several structures, injuring five workers and killing one; in October of the following year, an oiler suffered a fall that resulted in a fractured skull.[397] In early 1923, Shockoe Creek flooded, covering the floors of the shops with a foot of water. A resultant short pause in production on four Z-4 class engines (2-8-8-2) for the Northern Pacific Railway on account of an act of nature was certainly understandable. What was not understandable, however, was the fact that work recommenced on the engines without notifying the railroad, therefore not allowing for many standard tests on the part of the purchaser's own inspectors. Further issues in shipping these engines to Minnesota, and the incessant malfunctions that plagued the engines thereafter, dampened the enthusiasm from several longtime customers and saw an outright end to any further Richmond orders on behalf of the Northern Pacific.[398] Productivity suffered further when, on the evening of July 30, 1923, Shockoe Creek overflowed yet again, submerging some portions of the shop floors under as much as six feet of water and resulting in a complete shutdown of all operations for over a week, as all 3,000 men engaged in locomotive construction at the time were redirected to pump water or inspect and repair damaged machinery and products.[399]

The last ALCO order fulfilled in Richmond, Order No. R-389 for a single 4-6-2 locomotive for the Louisville, Henderson & St. Louis Railroad, left the

Southern Railway No. 1396, 1926, 4-6-2. *Nathan Vernon Madison.*

plant in September 1927, a year during which only 60 locomotives shipped. For most of its existence as a component of the American Locomotive Company, the Richmond Locomotive Works was maintained as a separate corporation due to the bonded debts ALCO had incurred in absorbing the Richmond Works; once the bonds reached maturity on April 1, 1929, the Richmond Locomotive Works was officially dissolved as a corporate entity.[400]

Two years before the last locomotive left the Richmond Branch, a familial connection that had existed since the firm's founding in 1865 ended with the resignation from ALCO in 1925 of Chester Alexander Delaney, son of Matthew Delaney and cousin to Alexander. Within a few short years of leaving the Richmond Locomotive Works in 1898 and relocating to the Dickson Locomotive Works in Scranton, Chester would be reunited with his hometown, in a manner of speaking, as Dickson was one of the firms that was combined to create ALCO in 1901. Following a tenure at ALCO Dickson that lasted until February 1908, Chester transferred to Chicago, accepting a promotion to serve as ALCO's western sales representative. This role, which he retained until his retirement, carried him across the country as he represented ALCO at various industry functions, including acting as the chief exhibitor for the firm at several annual Traveling Engineer's Association conventions.[401] During his years in Richmond, Chester married twice: first Mary W. Bigelow, daughter of Richmond-based attorney Woodbury B. Bigelow, a marriage that resulted in no children. Chester's second marriage, to Abbie Nance Day, produced three daughters—it was at the home of one of these daughters, Mrs. Allan P. Turner, that Chester Alexander Delaney died, in Flushing, New York, on November 7, 1935.[402]

ALCO, post-Richmond, would continue on for several decades. However, it was evident by the 1920s that the end of the Steam Age was fast approaching. The 1920s through the 1940s was a period of transitions for the company, as it struggled to survive in a changing marketplace; 1917 saw ALCO claim the 52nd position among the 200 largest industrial concerns in the United States. ALCO had declined to the 145th position by 1948, before dropping further in ensuing years and exiting the rolls entirely.[403]

A year after the closure of its Richmond Branch, ALCO was in an enviable position, having bested its longtime rival, Baldwin; ALCO claimed a 47 percent share of the locomotive manufacturing market, followed by Baldwin's 39 percent and the Lima Locomotive Works' 14 percent in 1928.[404] The succeeding years would see lows, particularly during the Great Depression, as well as highs, as ALCO diversified into mass production of diesel locomotives beginning in 1931 and tank contracts during World War II. In 1948, a century after the founding of the Schenectady Locomotive Works, the central precursor firm to ALCO, the company produced its final steam locomotive, a 2-8-4 engine for the Pittsburgh & Lake Erie Railroad, and thereafter produced only diesel locomotives. Between 1848 and 1948, all of ALCO's constituent facilities, during their individual and combined existences, produced over 75,000 steam locomotives.[405] In 1955, ALCO reorganized itself as Alco Products (Alco) to further demonstrate its diversification from locomotive production alone. Alco constructed the United States' first non-experimental nuclear reactor at the Army Nuclear Power Program's Fort Belvoir station in Virginia (first activated in 1957, decommissioned in 1973), as well as further reactors in the years that followed. A range of products including oil refinement equipment, heat exchangers for both land-based reactors and submarine use, and even M-47 and M-48 tanks during the Korean War made up much of Alco's output in the 1950s. The overseas diesel-electric locomotive market proved a boon for Alco, with 1958 seeing the company's market share in that arena reaching upward of 80 percent.[406] Following a merger with the Studebaker Corporation in 1967, locomotive production soon ceased entirely, and all locomotive designs were sold to its one-time subsidiary the Montreal Locomotive Works.[407] What remains today of the American Locomotive Company is largely in the form of patents, with many of its engine designs still being used by a large number of companies that have purchased rights to them in the ensuing years. A number of Alco patents were eventually purchased by the Beloit, Wisconsin–based Fairbanks Morse Defense, a supplier of engines and propulsion systems to the U.S. Navy, which to this day (2022) carries the FM ALCO 251F diesel engine model and is the "sole OEM [Original Equipment Manufacturer] for the ALCO engine product line."[408]

7

LEGACIES

1927 TO THE PRESENT

While the hammers may have fallen silent and the machinery come to a halt, the firm that over the years was known by a handful of names—Metropolitan Iron Works, the Tanner & Delaney Engine Company, the Richmond Locomotive and Machine Works, and lastly ALCO Richmond—survived in the memory of the general populace as Richmond continued to cede its position as a center of southern industry, and particularly in the minds of its former workmen, who, when looking back at their tenures, collectively referred to the plant affectionately and simply as "The Works." Many of the younger workmen transitioned to other industries that could make use of their skills, such as the several iron foundries within city limits still operating, including the legendary Tredegar Iron Works, the Old Dominion Iron and Nail Works on Bell Isle, and the OK Foundry across the James River in old Manchester. Many of the industrial concerns the Richmond Chamber of Commerce praised in 1903 began to fade only a few decades later. Some were temporarily rejuvenated by government contracts during the two world wars, only to be followed by a quick downturn, as smaller consumer goods manufacturers and an ever-increasing service industry supplanted much of the heavy and capital goods industry that the Richmond Locomotive Works had epitomized. Tredegar, in operation since 1837, closed in 1957 due largely to a shrinking market for its product and its failure to transition to steel; Old Dominion Iron and Nails closed in 1972. Many of the smaller iron works across the city were forced to either modernize or close in the face of environmental regulations issued by the newly established Environmental Protection Agency. While some, such as the OK Foundry, were able to transition to cleaner-burning furnaces and meet EPA requirements, others were not. Other major, industrial endeavors were receding as well. In 1962, Albemarle Paper Manufacturing purchased Pennsylvania-based Ethyl Corporation and, with an increased emphasis on petroleum additives and other chemical goods, closed its Richmond paper mills within a few short years.[409] In 1952, the Richmond Cedar Works placed its Richmond premises for sale but continued to operate in other locations, following the company's 1967 purchase by a Danville tobacco concern, which used the name to primarily produce, of all things, wooden ice cream machines. By 1990, the Richmond Cedar Works, operating only as a brand name by that point, had ceased to exist.[410]

Accessories Plant

On June 30, 1949, when the ALCO Accessories Plant at 1301 Boulevard was officially closed, the property was offered for sale at a suggested price of $300,000 (around $3.6 million in 2022), formally declaring the end of ALCO's nearly half-century presence in Richmond. The liquidation of the facility was necessary, according to C.D. Jeffress, manager of the site during its last years, "due to the fact that the demand for steam locomotive parts… has reached the point where it is not economical to operate this plant."[411] The editorial section of the Monday, July 4, 1949 edition of the *Richmond News Leader*, in a lengthy column chronicling the history of the company and its associated buildings, took note of the importance of the facility's role in Richmond industry while also acknowledging that, for better or for worse, it indeed belonged to an era whose time had long since passed.

> *Regret is natural, but there should be no lament. The elimination of this and of a score of other plants in the United States, along with the scores of locomotive railroad shops, is part of the economical transfer of American rail transportation from steam to oil—from the old-time, roaring, pounding engine to a new Diesel power.…Every community that loses an establishment in this process must realize that the closing of a shop or of a locomotive works is part of its contribution to the survival of cheap transportation in America.*[412]

As operations ceased in Shockoe Valley and portions of the former ALCO Richmond plant faced demolition in the late 1920s and early 1930s, the

Accessories Plant on Boulevard continued to produce accoutrements for use on ALCO locomotives on a periodic basis. Between March and December 1931, the Accessories Plant was leased to the Chevrolet Commercial Body Division of General Motors. Commercial truck bodies were fabricated at the plant before being attached to premade chassis and then shipped out, at a rate of 100 monthly, to customers in southern markets; following the end of the lease, GM acquired larger, more adequate facilities for its needs elsewhere.[413] ALCO's own production continued on a haphazard basis, with former workmen offered renewed employment in the event of an order being received. In February 1933, when a contract for power reverse gears for use on locomotives was secured, the company decided that "some of the old men would be recalled" to fulfill the order.[414] George Gurry, who had become the managing director of ALCO Richmond in 1911, remained as such, now overseeing the company's sole remaining operating outpost in the city. In 1933, Gurry finally resigned, and he was succeeded by Julius Kindervater, a longtime ALCO employee and mechanical engineer in his own right with several patents to his name, including one for staybolt connectors manufactured at the Accessories Plant. Kindervater was succeeded by Jeffress.[415] On the afternoon of July 25, 1942, at the age of 77, George Gurry passed away at his home in Gloucester Point, Virginia.[416]

On April 8, 1936, as ALCO's presence on the site continued to dwindle, the property was leased by the Brooks Transfer and Storage Company.[417] Founded in 1878 by John Williams Brooks with a single horse and wagon to offer freight transportation for both private and commercial customers, the company expanded briefly into a horse-drawn passenger line along the Mayo Bridge across the James River before refocusing on the hauling of goods and other freight. As early as 1914, Brooks' horse-drawn wagons began to be replaced with trucks, a process that continued until the last horse and wagon were sold in the early 1920s. From their initial garage and warehouse at 6 South Linden Street, Brooks' trucks became something of a celebrity around the state themselves, with the sides adorned with paintings of important events and personages from throughout Virginia history. During the Great Depression, Brooks' management, now in the hands of the founder's sons, James A. Brooks and C. Fair Brooks, understood that many businesses would be ordering on an as-needed basis, in order to prevent retaining large inventories in such lean pecuniary times. The overnight freight deliveries Brooks soon began to offer aided in the company's survival, and growth, during the Depression and early years of World War II. In 1932, Brooks opened its first out-of-state terminal in New York, soon to

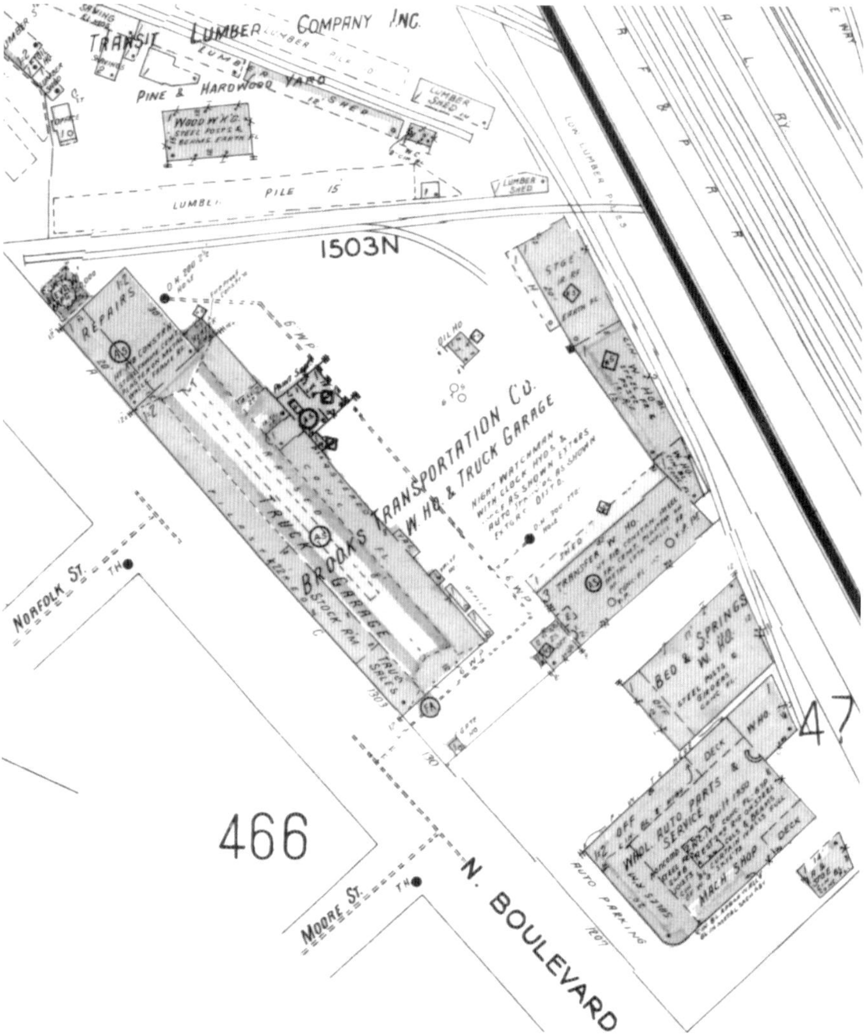

Brooks Transportation Company, at the former ALCO Accessories Plant site, 1952. Sanborn Insurance Maps. *Library of Congress, Geography and Map Division, Sanborn Maps Collection.*

be followed by those in Philadelphia, Baltimore, and Washington, as well as others throughout Virginia's western regions, including Roanoke and Lynchburg. It was at this time that the company formed a subsidiary branch, the Brooks Transportation Company, beginning with four new tractor trailers, to expand into even heavier commercial conveyance. To house and maintain an ever-increasing fleet of trucks, the now-seven-acre plot and easily converted ALCO shops of the Accessories Plant were ideal, and

Top: Brooks Transportation Company, at the former ALCO Accessories Plant site, 1953. *Courtesy of Jeff Brooks.*

Bottom: Bow Tie Cinemas–Movieland—formerly the ALCO Accessories Plant, 2022. *Nathan Vernon Madison.*

evidently proved quite satisfactory, as the firm purchased the site outright in 1950, following ALCO's offer of sale the previous year.

Brooks augmented the facility to suit its particular needs, with the central building of the Accessories Plant redesigned to serve as a truck garage; a repair shop on the far northern end; and stock rooms and the firm's sales offices located on the southwest corner, facing Boulevard. Additional offices and warehousing space were also maintained at 1224 West Broad Street by

1953, a year in which the company employed 752 employees (566 of those were drivers), with 600 trucks traversing approximately 8.5 million miles annually.[418] Brooks maintained a presence at Boulevard and Leigh until 1982, at which point the company relocated to Virginia Beach. The former pattern shop, at the corner of Leigh, was demolished at this time due to its being riddled with asbestos.[419] In 2009, a renovated and restored former Accessories Plant became the home of Bow Tie Cinemas' Movieland at Boulevard Square; the 17-screen attraction contains numerous paintings, photographs, and signage relating the history of the Richmond Locomotive Works.

The Richmond Works

The Shockoe Valley plant was certainly capable of being refitted and retooled for other functions, as demonstrated during World War I; unfortunately, no such purposes aligned with ALCO's vision of its own corporate future. It had already closed a majority of its locomotive shops, and those that did survive were increasingly focused on new industries and diversified production lines, not least of which the construction of diesel locomotives, an industry for which Richmond could boast neither adequate facilities nor a specialized workforce. While any useful machinery was stripped out and shipped to other ALCO facilities, a skeleton crew continued to operate out of the administrative offices, managing what was left of ALCO's holdings in the city (at this point, namely the Accessories Plant), as late as 1930.[420] Several fires and demolition of select structures occurred throughout the 1930s, and ALCO planned to raze the entire site in late 1937 if no buyers presented themselves.[421]

The spring of 1938 witnessed three new industries purchase or lease properties across the former Locomotive Works premises, rescuing it from complete destruction, contracts all negotiated by longtime ALCO Richmond attorney Murray McGuire. On April 21, 1938, president of the Richmond Engineering Company and former ALCO Richmond employee Ernst Farley announced his intention to construct "the largest steel fabricating plant in the southeast" with its purchase of five of the remaining structures on-site. Richmond Engineering was founded in 1914, initially based at 12 South 8th Street in the city's downtown, before relocating in 1917 to a two-block plant at 1305 Brook Avenue (now Brook Road), primarily focused on steel fabrication and the manufacture of everything from smoke stacks, radiators, and boilers to septic, oil, and gasoline tanks and various types of chutes and hoppers; many of the water tanks that

Richmond Engineering Company, Brook Road facility, 1917. *Courtesy of Shamrock Environmental, 2022.*

adorned Richmond landmarks such as the American National Bank and the Thalhimer's department store were manufactured by the company.[422] While the Locomotive Works' eastern edge, its erecting shop, had bordered 7th Street, most of this building was removed, with Richmond Engineering operating primarily in new facilities that paralleled it on the other side of 7th, in a corner bordered by the intersections of Hospital and Valley Road; the ALCO office building built in 1909 remained, which Richmond Engineering used for the same purposes. About a week after Richmond Engineering's announcement, McGuire helped cement another purchase on April 28, as Richmond Structural Steel agreed to purchase six acres, including the remnants of ALCO Richmond's smith and hammer shop. Richmond Structural Steel, a firm founded in 1905 and originally located between Broad and Marshall Streets on 18th and later occupying a portion of the defunct Trigg Shipbuilding Company, produced largely ornamental and (as the name suggests) structural steel and iron products, with hopes to expand into trusses and other, larger offerings given its newly acquired, 40,000-square-foot workspace.[423] Additionally, following the lease of a 50,000-square-foot building to the east of Richmond Engineering, the newly chartered Dixie Container Corporation began production of corrugated cardboard boxes and other shipping paraphernalia beginning in May 1938.[424] The section of the former Works between Richmond Engineering's complex and the 5th Street viaduct, formerly home to the Works' boiler, tank, and machine shops and iron foundry, was, as of 1939, occupied by several tobacco warehouses operated by cigarette manufacturers Larus & Bros. Company.[425]

During World War II, the Richmond Engineering Company joined DuPont, Reynolds Metals, and other prominent Richmond companies in

Former ALCO Richmond site, with Richmond Engineering Company facility. Visible is the ALCO Richmond office building, 1938. *Courtesy of Shamrock Environmental, 2022.*

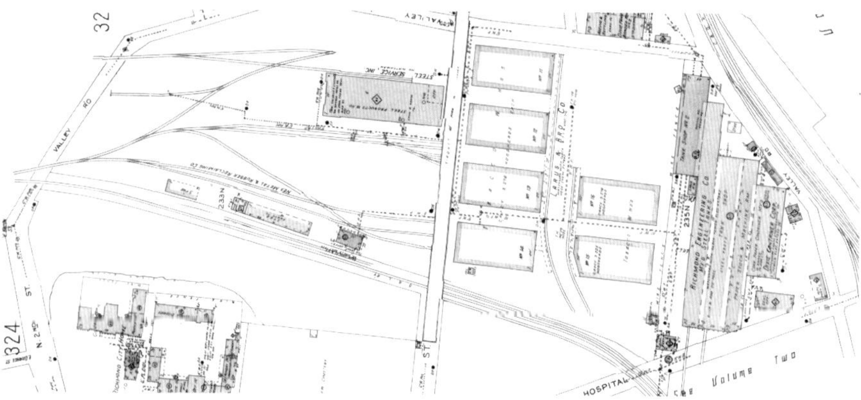

Richmond Engineering Company, at the former ALCO Richmond site, 1952. Sanborn Insurance Maps. *Library of Congress, Geography and Map Division, Sanborn Maps Collection.*

securing government contracts, producing not only various types of storage tanks and components for munitions but also transverse bulkheads, which aid in the creation of airtight compartments on naval vessels. The welds needed for bomb heads, tank hulls, and other war materiel were supplied, not by longtime steel workers but rather by women, newly entering the engineering sector during the war years, Richmond's very own "Rosie the Rivetters." So many women were employed at the plant, upward of 300 at its peak, that a women's personnel director, Blanche Kidd Satterfield, wife of Congressman David E. Satterfield Jr., was hired.[426] In the spring of 1942, portions of the remaining ALCO Richmond plant were dismantled and shipped to Youngstown, Ohio, rebuilt there to produce tanks for use in the European theater by the General American Transportation Company.[427]

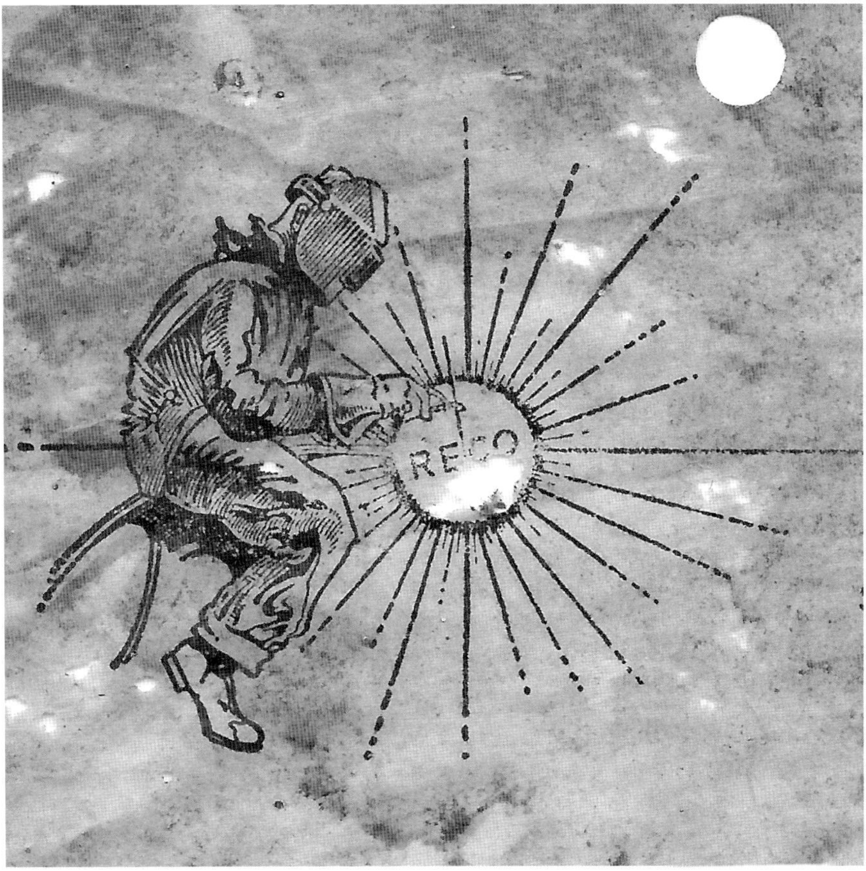

RECO Letterhead, circa 1950. *Nathan Vernon Madison.*

Between the 1950s and the 1970s, the former Works site was increasingly dominated by the Richmond Engineering Company, which by the 1990s had renamed itself simply to RECO. The subsequent decades were times of diversification for the company. While still producing storage tanks of varying and often enormous size, RECO entered the biodiesel fuel and soil reclamation markets under a subsidiary named RECO Biotechnology. Using a bioremediation process to cleanse soil formerly polluted by petroleum for safe use in various construction and filling projects across the state, RECO Biotechnology produced more than 500,000 tons worth of reclaimed soil between 1994 and 2022.[428]

As of 2022, Shamrock Environmental, having purchased the RECO Biotechnology division some years prior, operates the site and continues to

Former ALCO Richmond office building, circa 1950. *Courtesy of Shamrock Environmental, 2022.*

focus on soil reclamation. The former ALCO office building, now attached to the Shamrock Environmental offices and unoccupied at the moment, has been renovated and refurbished. During one of these refurbishments, workers removing ceiling panels revealed the intricately inlaid ceiling of the room as it originally existed in 1909; this ceiling has been preserved—one of the few reminders of the structure's historical importance.

In 1952, Southern Railway president Harry A. Debutts donated one of the company's recently retired steam engines to the Smithsonian Institution, then in the initial stages of planning much-needed expansions. The engine selected was No. 1401, a 132-ton Pacific 4-6-2 locomotive completed at ALCO Richmond in July 1926.[429] Aside from being among the last Richmond locomotives purchased by the Southern, No. 1401 held a prominent place in American history, as it was one of several engines used in April 1945 to pull President Franklin D. Roosevelt's funeral train from Warm Springs, Georgia, to Washington, D.C. For nearly nine years following Debutts's donation, No. 1401 remained in storage in Alexandria. By the spring of 1962, it had been fully restored and removed to Washington during the construction of its new home, the Smithsonian Institution's Museum of History and Technology (today's National Museum of American History), which opened two years later. Police motorcycles and squad cars escorted No. 1401 during its slow, one-and-a-half-mile, 22-hour journey to the museum, for which a tractor-trailer with 55 wheels and reinforced manhole covers with steel plating along the route were necessary.[430] No. 1401 has remained on display since the museum's January 1964 opening and has been viewed by hundreds of millions of

Above: Former ALCO Richmond administrative office building, 2022. *Nathan Vernon Madison.*

Left: Former ALCO Richmond administrative office building, 2022. *Nathan Vernon Madison.*

Shamrock Environmental, with remnants of rails, 2022. *Nathan Vernon Madison.*

Southern Railway No. 1401, 1926, 4-6-2, on display at the Smithsonian Institution's Museum of National History. *Smithsonian Institution, National Museum of American History website Steam Locomotive, Southern Railway 1401.*

Richmond Locomotive Works. *From* Richmond Virginia: The City on the James, *1903.*

visitors in that span—a testament to the city's industrial past and the labors of the thousands upon thousands of men who, over the course of 60 years, made their livelihoods at "the Works."

During the long transition from the old Richmond to the new, many of the old-timers of ALCO Richmond retained pride in their time at the Works. While interviewing several former ALCO Richmond employees in the late 1960s, locomotive historian William E. Warden Jr. noted they all reminisced fondly about their efforts, the quality of work they produced and the management styles of company leaders such as Columbus Lassiter and others. These interviews undoubtedly left their mark on Warden—after speaking to former ALCO Richmond workers such as riveter Everett Grant, machinist L.J. Peyonet, and steamfitter Thomas Green, he concluded, that when speaking to such men:

> *You are with these men in the steamy cacophonous shops. You hear the clunk of the huge hydraulic riveting machine fabricating mud rings and the staccato blows of a steam hammer shaping white hot billets of steel into side rods. You smell grease and steel and smoky fires. You watch the 40-horsepower planer throw chips as thick as a man's thumb from the emerging engine bed of a Virginian mallet or gape in slack-jawed wonderment as an overhead crane effortlessly carries the engine bed to another machine. You see workers everywhere—purposeful, prideful, sweaty, greasy men—and, like them, you are tempted to agree that "Richmond built the world's best locomotives."*[431]

NOTES

Abbreviations

Journals

RH	*Railroad History*
HSB	*The Railway and Locomotive History Society Bulletin*
IAM	*Monthly Journal of the International Association of Machinists*
VMHB	*Virginia Magazine of History and Biography*

Institutions

LVA	Library of Virginia
VMHC	Virginia Museum of History & Culture
VM	Valentine Museum
SI	Smithsonian Institution

1. Rails Come to Richmond and Early Engine Manufacturers, 1810–1865

1. Charles W. Turner, and Charles F. Turner, "The Early Railroad Movement in Virginia," *VMHB* 55, no. 4 (October 1947): 350.
2. Ibid.
3. Ibid.; Sean Patrick Adams, *Old Dominion, New Commonwealth—Coal, Politics, and Economy in Antebellum America* (Baltimore: Johns Hopkins University Press, 2004), 165.

4. Turner and Turner, "Early Railroad Movement," 351; Nathan Vernon Madison, "Richmond's Industrial Heritage," in *Society for Industrial Archeology 47th Annual Conference Guidebook* (Houghton: SIA/Michigan Technological University, 2018), 6.
5. Frederick C. Gamst and Marilou Gamst, "Virginia's First Railroad, on Falling Creek, about 1810," *RH* no. 168 (Spring 1993): 5.
6. Ibid., 6.
7. Harry M. Ward and Richard E. Greer Jr., *Richmond During the Revolution, 1775–83* (Charlottesville: University Press of Virginia, 1977), 22; Gamst and Gamst, "Virginia's First Railroad," 6.
8. Gamst and Gamst, "Virginia's First Railroad," 7; H.W. Flournoy, ed., *Calendar of Virginia State Papers and Other Manuscripts*, vol. 10 (New York: Kraus Reprint Corporation, 1968 [1892]), 201.
9. Gamst and Gamst, "Virginia's First Railroad," 7.
10. Ibid., 8.
11. Ibid., 8.
12. Ibid., 9.
13. F.R. Wadleigh, "Story of the Richmond Coal Fields," 34213, Richmond Coal Basin Project File, 1811–1953, LVA, 11.
14. Ibid., 21.
15. Ibid., 22.; Turner and Turner, "Early Railroad Movement," 355.
16. *Richmond Enquirer*, December 24, 1833.
17. *Phenix Gazette*, February 12, 1830.
18. Turner and Turner, "Early Railroad Movement," 353.
19. Gamst and Gamst, "Virginia's First Railroad," 13.
20. Turner and Turner, "Early Railroad Movement," 361–62.
21. Laura E. Armitage, "Louisa Railroad—1836–1850; Virginia Central Railroad—1850–1868," *HSB* no. 65 (October 1944): 59.
22. Stuart Bowe Medlin, "The York River Railroad: 1851–1881" (master's thesis, University of Richmond, 1968).
23. *Poor's Manual of Railroads* (New York: H.V. & H.W. Poor, 1877), 354.
24. *Virginia Argus*, November 30, 1805; *Richmond Enquirer*, March 22, 1808.
25. John H. White Jr., "Richmond Locomotive Builders," *RH*, no. 130 (Spring 1974): 68; *Richmond Enquirer*, August 7, 1818.
26. White, "Richmond Locomotive Builders," 68; Richard E. Prince, *Seaboard Air Line Railway: Steam Boats, Locomotives, and History* (Bloomington: Indiana University Press, 2000), 13.
27. Prince, *Seaboard Air Line Railway*, 10–11.

28. *United States Congressional Serial Set*, vol. 345 (Washington: U.S. Government Printing Office, n.d.), 241.
29. White, "Richmond Locomotive Builders," 68; *Richmond Daily Whig*, June 16, 1843; *Staunton Spectator and General Advertiser*, June 22, 1843.
30. *Richmond Enquirer*, February 9, 1858.
31. *Richmond Enquirer*, October 21, 1834.
32. *Congressional Serial Set*, 345:241.
33. White, "Richmond Locomotive Builders," 69; Agreement between Talbott Brothers and the Shockoe Manufacturing Company January 30, 1840, Talbott & Brother Records, Mss3 T1425 a, VMHC.
34. Apprenticeship Contracts, 1854–1859, Talbott & Brother Records, VMHC.
35. White, "Richmond Locomotive Builders," 69; *Annual Reports of Internal Improvements Companies of Virginia to the Board of Public Works 1856* (Richmond, VA: Board of Public Works, 1856), 862.
36. Andrea Mehrlander, *The Germans of Charleston, Richmond, and New Orleans During the Civil War* (Berlin: Walter de Gruyter GmbH & Co., 2011), 47, 64; *Richmond Enquirer*, November 17, 1848.
37. *Richmond Daily Times*, March 5, 1852.
38. *Daily Times*, April 8, 1852; *Richmond Daily Whig*, December 5, 1856.
39. F.W. Beers, *Illustrated Atlas of the city of Richmond, Va.* (Richmond, VA: F.W. Beers, 1877), map. https://www.loc.gov/item/2005630891/; *Daily Dispatch*, May 10, 1852.
40. *Daily Dispatch*, July 11, 1853.
41. White, "Richmond Locomotive Builders," 69; *Daily Dispatch*, April 11, 1855.
42. *Daily Dispatch*, June 30, 1852; *Daily Dispatch*, March 12, 1856.
43. *Richmond Enquirer*, November 19, 1858.
44. *Richmond Enquirer*, July 10, 1860.
45. Colin Maggs, *Steam Trains: The Magnificent History of Britain's Locomotives from Stephenson's Rocket to BR's Evening Star* (Gloucestershire, UK: Amberley Publishing, 2015), 15.
46. Robert Sobel, *Panic on Wall Street: A History of America's Financial Disasters* (New York: Collier Books, 1968), 32–76; Larry Schweikart, "Specie, Hard Money, and 'Suspension,'" in *The Encyclopedia of American Business History and Biography: Banking and Finance to 1913*, ed. Larry Schweikart (New York: Facts on File, 1990), 445.
47. Charles B. Dew, *Ironmaker to the Confederacy: Joseph R. Anderson and the Tredegar Iron Works*, 2nd ed. (Richmond: Library of Virginia, 1999), 8–12.

48. Gregg D. Kimball, *American City, Southern Place: A Cultural History of Antebellum Richmond* (Athens: University of Georgia Press, 2000), 182; Nathan Vernon Madison, *Tredegar Iron Works: Richmond's Foundry on the James* (Charleston, SC: The History Press, 2015), 58.
49. *American Railroad Journal* (United States: J.H. Schultz, 1853), 567.
50. White, "Richmond Locomotive Builders," 71.
51. Matthew Delaney, Valentine's Richmond History Vertical Files, VM.
52. *Virginia Reports, 1730–1880* (Charlottesville, VA: The Michie Company, 1902), 575.
53. *Lynchburg Virginian*, December 25, 1851.
54. Agreement, July 1, 1854, Tredegar Iron Works Records, 1801–1957, Accession 23881, 24808. Series VIII—Subseries 6: Estate of Joseph Reid Anderson, Box 1210, LVA; "Inflation Calculator," U.S. Official Inflation Data, Alioth Finance, July 29, 2022, https://www.officialdata.org/. All other sources for inflation are attributed to this source; due to the rapid inflation experienced in 2022, amounts should be considered approximate in nature.
55. *Daily Dispatch*, January 13, 1855.
56. John H. White Jr., Peter A. Hansen, and Dan Cupper, "Histories of the Individual Firms," *RH* no. 197 (Fall-Winter 2007): 80.
57. *Annual Reports of Internal Improvements*, 862.
58. Vertical Files, Matthew Delaney, VM.
59. Dew, *Ironmaker to the Confederacy*, 288.
60. White, "Richmond Locomotive Builders," 72.
61. Sobel, *Panic on Wall Street*, 77–114.
62. Dew, *Ironmaker to the Confederacy*, 35, 127.
63. *Alexandria Gazette*, May 19, 1863.
64. *Richmond Enquirer*, May 31, 1861.
65. Mehrlander, *Germans of Charleston*, 64.
66. Michael B. Chesson, *Richmond After the War: 1865–1890* (Richmond: Virginia State Library, 1981), 57.
67. Ibid., 59.
68. Ibid., 60.
69. Virginius Dabney, *Richmond: The Story of a City* (Garden City, NJ: Doubleday, 1976), 225; W. David Lewis, "Joseph Bryan and the Virginia Connection in the Industrial Development of Northern Alabama," *VMHB* 98, no. 4 (October 1990): 614.
70. Chesson, *Richmond After the War*, 71.

2. The Metropolitan Iron Works/Tanner & Delaney Engine Company, 1865–1887

71. *Richmond Times-Dispatch*, March 24, 1910.
72. Joicey Haw Lindsay, "Henrico County, Virginia, Naturalizations, 1844–1858," *Magazine of Virginia Genealogy* 22, no. 4 (November 1984): 14; *Richmond Times-Dispatch*, March 24, 1910.
73. *Richmond Dispatch*, April 1, 1900.
74. *Times-Dispatch*, March 24, 1910.
75. White, "Richmond Locomotive Builders," 86.
76. *Richmond Dispatch*, August 7, 1898.
77. Lieutenant Colonel Jerome A. Watrous, ed., *Memoirs of Milwaukie County: From The Earliest Historical Times Down To The Present, Including a Genealogical and Biographical Record of Representative Families in Milwaukie County*, vol. 2 (Madison, WI: Western Historical Association, 1909), 77.
78. Ibid.
79. Undated research notes relating to William E. Tanner by John H. White Jr., NMAH.AC.0523, John H. White Jr. Railroad Reference Collection, Smithsonian Institution, Washington, D.C.
80. Ibid.
81. *Daily Dispatch*, February 4, 1869.
82. *Alexandria Gazette*, December 5, 1866.
83. *Daily Dispatch*, December 27, 1865
84. *Daily Dispatch*, September 19, 1870.
85. *Daily Dispatch*, August 2, 1869.
86. Watrous, *Memoirs of Milwaukie County*, 78.
87. Ibid., 77.
88. Staff of Forest Home Cemetery, Milwaukee, Wisconsin, phone conversation/research request with author, October 25, 2022.
89. *Daily Dispatch*, January 4, 1871; James Mercer Garnett, *University of Virginia: Its History, Influence, Equipment and Characteristics, with Biographical Sketches and Portraits of Founders, Benefactors, Officers and Alumni*, vol. 1 (Princeton, NJ: Princeton University, 1904), 454.
90. Garnett, *University of Virginia*, 454; *Daily Dispatch*, February 18, 1876.
91. *Daily Dispatch*, September 19, 1870.
92. Ibid.
93. *Alexandria Gazette*, February 28, 1872; *Daily State Journal*, February 29, 1872.

94. *Daily State Journal*, June 27, 1872.
95. *Daily Dispatch*, March 21, 1871; *Daily Dispatch*, March 24, 1871; *Daily State Journal*, June 27, 1872.
96. *Daily Dispatch*, May 26, 1883; *Daily Dispatch*, July 15, 1883.
97. *Richmond Dispatch*, December 4, 1884.
98. *Richmond Dispatch*, January 25, 1885.
99. *Alexandria Gazette*, April 30, 1885.
100. *Daily State Journal*, January 6, 1873.
101. White Collection, SI.
102. *Daily Dispatch*, June 15, 1877.
103. *Richmond Dispatch*, February 16, 1875.
104. Laura E. Armitage, "Richmond and Alleghany Railroad," *HSB*, no. 88 (May 1953): 59.
105. *Daily Dispatch*, August 13, 1875.
106. *Daily Dispatch*, August 16, 1879.
107. *Daily Dispatch*, November 12, 1881.
108. *Staunton Spectator*, November 15, 1881; *Jeffersonian Republican*, November 16, 1881.
109. *Richmond Dispatch*, March 29, 1882.
110. *Daily Dispatch*, July 15, 1882; *Railroad Gazette* 15 (August 3, 1883): 515; James P. Woods, *The Industries of Richmond: Her Trade, Commerce, Manufactures and Representative Establishments* (Richmond, VA: Metropolitan Publishing, 1886), 49.
111. *Daily Dispatch*, July 15, 1882.
112. *Richmond Dispatch*, June 9, 1886.
113. Betsy Hunter Bradley, *The Works: The Industrial Architecture of the United States* (New York: Oxford University Press, 1999), 16.
114. Ibid., 21.
115. Ibid., 26.
116. *Railroad Gazette* 15 (August 3, 1883): 515.
117. *Staunton Spectator*, February 25, 1885.
118. Mike McKnight and Robert T. Rhode, "Captain William Edward Cole and His Pole Road Locomotives of the American South," *Engineers & Engines* 64, no. 6 (April/May 2019): 3.
119. Ibid., 5.
120. Ibid.
121. Advertisement for Tanner & Delaney Pole Road Locomotives, 1886, White Collection, SI.
122. McKnight and Rhode, "Captain William Edward Cole," 13.

123. Advertisement for Tanner & Delaney Pole Road Locomotives, 1886, White Collection, SI.
124. Ibid.
125. White, "Richmond Locomotive Builders," 75.
126. *Richmond Dispatch*, August 7, 1898.
127. *Richmond Dispatch*, January 6, 1887.
128. *Times Dispatch*, February 17, 1903.
129. Ibid.
130. White, "Richmond Locomotive Builders," 87; *Times-Dispatch*, February 17, 1903.
131. *Richmond Dispatch*, February 13, 1890; *Times-Dispatch*, February 17, 1903.
132. *Richmond Dispatch*, May 15, 1887.
133. Robert Alonzo Brock and Virgil Anson Lewis, *Virginia and Virginians: Eminent Virginians* (Richmond, VA: H.H. Hardesty, 1888), 656; Vertical File: Matthew Delaney, VM.
134. *Times Dispatch*, March 24, 1910.
135. Robert R. Nuckols, *A History of the Government of the City of Richmond, Virginia and Sketch of Those Who Administer Its Affairs* (Richmond, VA: Williams Printing Company, 1899), 58.
136. *Times Dispatch*, March 24, 1910.
137. *Railway and Locomotive Engineering* 11 (November 1898): 512; P.M. Arthur, et al., *Brotherhood of Locomotive Engineer's Monthly Journal* 22 (1888): 1099.

3. The Richmond Locomotive and Machine Works, 1887–1901

138. *Richmond Dispatch*, November 10, 1887.
139. Brian Burns, *Gilded Age Richmond: Gaiety, Greed & Lost Cause Mania* (Charleston, SC: The History Press, 2017), 54; J.H. Chataigne, *The Chesapeake & Ohio Railway Directory, 1881–1882* (Richmond, VA, 1881), 176.
140. *Daily Dispatch*, March 17, 1868.
141. *Richmond Dispatch*, August 2, 1887.
142. White, "Richmond Locomotive Builders," 76.
143. *Daily Times*, August 28, 1888.
144. U.S. Congress, House of Representatives, *Richmond Locomotive and Machine Works*, March 2, 1895, 53rd Cong., 3rd sess., 1895, Report No. 1982; *Richmond Times*, January 15, 1891.
145. Report No. 1982.
146. White, "Richmond Locomotive Builders," 75.

147. Some surviving records contain information about the number of locomotives produced each year; however, that only is the case through 1900, whereafter the most complete information is sorted by the number shipped from the Works each year. For the sake of consistency, I have decided to simply use shipment years throughout.
148. Minutes of the Richmond Locomotive Works, Account Book, 1899–1902, Joseph Bryan Papers, Mss1 B8407 b 132-200, VMHC.
149. John K. Brown and Samuel M. Vauclain, "Comments on the System and Shop Practices of the Baldwin Locomotive Works," *RH* no. 173 (Autumn 1995): 107.
150. John K. Brown, *The Baldwin Locomotive Works, 1831–1915* (Baltimore: Johns Hopkins University Press, 1995), 163.
151. Brown and Vauclain, "Comments on the System," 114.
152. John H. White Jr., *A History of the American Locomotive: Its Development, 1830–1880* (New York: Dover Publications, 1968), 30–32, 103; *United States Census Bureau, Tenth Census, Census Report, June 1, 1880: Manufactures* (Washington, D.C.: Government Printing Office, 1883), 51.
153. Brown and Vauclain, "Comments on the System," 125.
154. White, *History of the American Locomotive*, 98.
155. Ibid., 17.
156. *Tenth Census, Manufactures*, 47.
157. Bruce Laurie, *Artisans to Workers: Labor in Nineteenth Century America* (Urbana: University of Illinois Press, 1997), 16.
158. Louis P. Cain, Price V. Fishbank, and Paul Rhode, eds., *The Oxford Handbook of American Economic History*, vol. 2 (New York: Oxford University Press, 2018), 77.
159. Laurie, *Artisans to Workers*, 142, 149.
160. Peter J. Rachleff, *Black Labor in the South* (Philadelphia: Temple University Press, 1984), 142.
161. Claudia Miner, "The 1886 Convention of the Knights of Labor," *Phylon* 44, no. 2 (2nd Qtr., 1983): 149.
162. Laurie, *Artisans to Workers*, 156.
163. *Richmond Dispatch*, January 30, 1886.
164. *Richmond Dispatch*, October 30, 1886.
165. Nathan Vernon Madison, "Joseph P. Devine (d. 1890)," *Dictionary of Virginia Biography*, Library of Virginia, http://www.lva.virginia.gov.
166. *Richmond Dispatch*, May 15, 1887.
167. James M. Lindgren, "'First and Foremost a Virginian': Joseph Bryan and the New South Economy," *VMHB* 96, no. 2 (April 1988): 178.

168. *Richmond Dispatch*, March 20, 1891.
169. *IAM* 3, no. 3 (Apr. 1891), 65.
170. *Engineering* 51 (January 30, 1891), 120; *Richmond Dispatch*, March 26, 1891.
171. *Roanoke Times*, May 10, 1891; *Richmond Times*, June 6, 1891.
172. *Richmond Times*, June 6, 1891.
173. *IAM* 3, no. 7 (August 1891): 198; *Richmond Times*, June 16, 1891.
174. *IAM* 3, no. 3 (June 1891): 130; *IAM* 3, no. 7 (August 1891): 198.
175. *Richmond Times*, October 9, 1892.
176. *Richmond Times*, November 18, 1892.
177. *Richmond Dispatch*, November 20, 1892.
178. Robert L. Frey, "Philadelphia & Reading Railroad," in *The Encyclopedia of American Business History and Biography: Railroads in the Nineteenth Century*, ed. Robert L. Frey (New York: Facts on File, 1988), 322.
179. Neil Shafer, Tom Sheehan, and Fred Reed, ed., *Panic Scrip of 1893, 1907 and 1914: An Illustrated Catalog of Emergency Monetary Issues* (Jefferson, NC: McFarland & Company, 2013), 7.
180. Albro Martin, "John Pierpont Morgan," in *The Encyclopedia of American Business History and Biography: Banking and Finance to 1913*, ed. Larry Schweikart (New York: Facts on File, 1990), 335.
181. Shafer, Sheehan, and Reed, *Panic Scrip of 1893*, 50–51.
182. *The Times*, August 15, 1893.
183. White, "Richmond Locomotive Builders," 79.
184. John W. Leonard., ed., *Men of America: A Biographical Dictionary of Contemporaries* (L.R. Hamersley & Company, New York, 1908), 1606.
185. White, "Richmond Locomotive Builders," 79.
186. *Catalogue of Exhibitors in the United States Sections of the International Universal Exposition Paris 1900* (Paris: Société Anonyme Des Imprimeries Lemercier, 1900), 177; White, 80.
187. White, "Richmond Locomotive Builders," 80.
188. Ibid., 76.
189. Ibid., 77; Angus Sinclair and John H. White Jr., *Development of the Locomotive Engine* (Cambridge, MA: MIT Press, 1970), 605.
190. T. Addison Busbey, ed. *Biographical Directory of the Railway Officials of America* (Chicago: The Railway Age, 1901), 203; Sinclair and White, *Development*, 605.
191. Sinclair and White, *Development*, 605.
192. Ibid.
193. *The Times*, January 1, 1901.
194. *Richmond Dispatch*, December 2, 1898.

195. *The Times*, November 1, 1899.
196. *The Times*, December 24, 1902.
197. Dabney, *Richmond*, 249; *The Times*, January 24, 1902.
198. *Richmond Dispatch*, January 4, 1903; *Richmond Dispatch*, January 14, 1903; *The Times*, January 14, 1903.
199. *Richmond Dispatch*, January 17, 1903.
200. *Times-Dispatch*, February 17, 1903.
201. *News Leader*, February 10, 1903.
202. *Times Dispatch*, June 23, 1905.
203. John Stewart Bryan, *Joseph Bryan: His Times, His Family, His Friends* (Richmond, VA: Whittet & Shepperson, 1935), 19.
204. Earle Dunford, *Richmond Times-Dispatch: The Story of a Newspaper* (Richmond, VA: Cadmus Publishing, 1995), prologue.
205. Maury Klein, *The Great Richmond Terminal* (Charlottesville: University Press of Virginia, 1970), 90; Robert C. Jones, *A History of Georgia Railroads* (Charleston, SC: The History Press, 2017), 14.
206. Brock and Lewis, *Virginia and Virginians*, 637.
207. Bryan, *Joseph Bryan*, 265; Notes of Assets, May 28, 1887, Accession Number 24882, Box 8, Folder 6, Bryan Family Papers, LVA.
208. White, "Richmond Locomotive Builders," 82; *American Machinist* 58, no. 10 (March 1923): 391.
209. William E. Warden Jr., "Richmond Locomotive Works," *Railroad Magazine*, September 1969, 21.
210. Ibid., 22.
211. *Iron Age* 111, no. 10 (March 1923): 719; *News Leader*, January 18, 1917.
212. Bryan, *Joseph Bryan*, 239.
213. L.B. Taylor, *Monsters of Virginia* (Mechanicsburg, VA: Stackpole Books, 2012), 24; Harry Kollatz Jr., "W.W. Pool: Richmond's Reputed Nosferatu," *Richmond Magazine*, October 2013, https://richmondmagazine.com.
214. *Anderson (SC) Intelligencer*, March 22, 1899; *Sessional Papers; Great Britain, Parliament, the House of Commons Diplomatic and Consular Reports—United States*, Her Majesty's Stationary Office, 1900, 15.
215. *Virginian-Pilot*, December 15, 1899.
216. Bryan Papers, 1889–1902, VMHC.
217. Ibid.
218. *Richmond Dispatch*, June 22, 1900.
219. *Washington Weekly-Post*, January 2, 1900; *Richmond Dispatch*, February 11, 1900; *The Times*, May 8, 1900.
220. *The Times*, November 4, 1900.

221. *The Times*, August 3, 1900.
222. *Indianapolis Journal*, January 13, 1901.
223. *El Paso Daily Herald*, January 29, 1901; *Richmond Dispatch*, Feburary 9, 1901.
224. Bryan Papers, 1889–1902, VMHC.

4. The American Locomotive Company—Richmond Works, 1901–1914

225. Richmond Chamber of Commerce [hereafter RCC], *Richmond Virginia: The City on the James* (Richmond, VA: George W. Engelhardt, 1903), 5.
226. Allen W. Moger, "Industrial and Urban Progress in Virginia from 1880 to 1900," *VMHB* 66, no. 3 (July 1958): 307.
227. Ibid., 309.
228. Chesson, *Richmond After the War*, 118.
229. Moger, "Industrial and Urban Progress," 315.
230. Bill Barber, *Tyrrell Timber: A History of the Branning Manufacturing Company and Richmond Cedar Works* (Middletown, VA: Bill Barber, 2021), 69; RCC, *Richmond, Virginia*, 105.
231. Moger, "Industrial and Urban Progress," 318.
232. Stephen Leibovic, "Southern Stove Works," National Register of Historic Places Nomination Form (Washington, D.C.: U.S. Department of the Interior, National Park Service, 2004), Section 8.
233. RCC, *Richmond, Virginia*, 98.
234. Moger, "Industrial and Urban Progress," 322.
235. Ibid., 323.
236. RCC, *Richmond, Virginia*, 77.
237. *Evening Times* (Washington, D.C.), May 7, 1901; J. Parker Lamb, *Perfecting the American Steam Engine* (Bloomington: Indiana University Press, 2003), 14; Brown, *Baldwin Locomotive Works*, 194; American Locomotive Company, *Growing with Schenectady* (New York: ALCO, 1948), 24; ALCO Annual Report 1902, 6.
238. *Times Dispatch*, June 10, 1904; ALCO Annual Report 1902, 16.
239. ALCO Annual Report 1902, 9.
240. ALCO Annual Report 1903, 7–8.
241. *Richmond Dispatch*, June 8, 1894.
242. Bryan, *Joseph Bryan*, 200.
243. Ibid., 267.

244. Oliver Zunz, *Making America Corporate, 1870–1920* (Chicago: University of Chicago Press, 1990), 4.
245. Ibid., 16.
246. Rachleff, *Black Labor*, 4.
247. Moger, "Industrial and Urban Progress," 313.
248. Bryan Papers, 1899–1902, VMHC.
249. Joseph Bryan to S.R. Callaway (December 28, 1903), Bryan Letterbook, 1903 March–December 31, Bryan Family Papers, Mss1 B8408 a 25, VMHC.
250. Joseph Bryan to A.J. Pitkin (December 29, 1903), VMHC.
251. Joseph Bryan to H.H. Doggett (June 18, 1903), VMHC.
252. Joseph Bryan to C.E. Patterson (March 27, 1903), VMHC.
253. Joseph Bryan to Rev. Beverly D. Tucker (October 26, 1903), VMHC.
254. Joseph Bryan to C.B. Denny (December 4, 1903), VMHC.
255. Bryan, *Joseph Bryan*, 269.
256. Ibid.
257. *The Times*, August 21, 1900.
258. *Richmond Dispatch*, October 18, 1900; *Richmond Dispatch*, December 1, 1900.
259. *The Times*, March 8, 1900; *Richmond Dispatch*, March 11, 1900.
260. *The Beneficial Society of the Richmond Locomotive and Machine Works* (Richmond, VA: Everett Waddey, 1889), 5.
261. Ibid., 11–14.
262. Ibid., 16.
263. Joseph Bryan to E.G. Williams (March 23, 1903), VMHC; Guide to the Board of Trustees of Memorial Hospital Records, Biographical/Historical Information, VCU.
264. Bryan to E.G. Williams (March 23, 1903), VMHC; Bryan to E.G. Williams (April 15, 1903), VMHC.
265. *Evening Journal*, September 29, 1905.
266. *News Leader*, March 30, 1903.
267. *Times-Dispatch*, July 3, 1904.
268. *Evening Journal*, July 27, 1912.
269. *Times-Dispatch*, June 20, 1903; *News Leader*, July 25, 1910.
270. *Richmond Dispatch*, June 22, 1902.
271. Joseph Bryan to S.R. Callaway (June 22, 1903), VMHC.
272. *The Times*, June 1, 1902.
273. White, "Richmond Locomotive Builders," 82.
274. *Times-Dispatch*, February 17, 1906.

275. *Richmond News Leader*, September 26, 1934.
276. *Times-Dispatch*, March 22, 1906.
277. *Times-Dispatch*, October 9, 1908.
278. *Newport News Daily Press*, March 22, 1907; April 6, 1907; May 19, 1907.
279. *Evening Journal*, February 5, 1908.
280. *Railway and Locomotive Engineering* 19, no. 7 (July 1906): 333; George S. May, "Autocar Company," in *The Encyclopedia of American Business History and Biography: The Automobile Industry*, ed. George S. May (New York: Facts on File, 1990), 23.
281. *News Leader*, May 7, 1908.
282. *Evening Journal*, November 24, 1908.
283. *News Leader*, December 23, 1908.
284. *Iron Age* 82, no. 26 (December 1908): 1917.
285. *Times-Dispatch*, July 26, 1942.
286. *The Railway Age and Northwestern Railroader* 27, no. 16 (April 21, 1899): 308; *Canadian Engineer* 11, no. 9 (September 1904): 279.
287. *Brown Alumni Monthly* 9, no. 10 (May 1909): 244.
288. *Official Proceedings of the Richmond Railroad Club* 15, no. 3 (January 1916): 1; *Richmond Virginian*, August 14, 1912.
289. *Times-Dispatch*, September 22, 1912.
290. Steven J. Ericson, "Importing Locomotives in Meiji Japan—International Business and Technology Transfer in the Railroad Industry" *Osiris* 13 (1998): 134.
291. Ibid., 138.
292. *Richmond Dispatch*, November 12, 1898; White, "Richmond Locomotive Builders," 81.
293. *Alumni Bulletin*, University of Virginia, Charlottesville, 1901, 65; *Times-Dispatch*, January 16, 1933.
294. *Richmond Times-Dispatch*, June 28, 1957.
295. Ibid.
296. Ibid.
297. Kurt Möller, "Swedish Steam with Richmond Plates," *HSB* 99 (October 1958): 55.
298. Ericson, "Importing Locomotives in Meiji Japan," 132.
299. Ibid., 145.
300. Ibid., 138.
301. Ibid., 153.
302. Ibid., 133.
303. *News Leader*, January 9, 1917.

304. *News Leader*, November 9, 1911.
305. Ibid.
306. *News Leader*, November 14, 1911; *Richmond Virginian*, November 18, 1911.
307. *Richmond Virginian*, November 21, 1911.
308. *Times Dispatch*, November 27, 1911.
309. *News Leader*, January 13, 1912.
310. *Evening Journal*, July 27, 1912.
311. *The Tradesman* 64, no. 8 (August 1910): 34.
312. *Machinists' Monthly Journal* 23, no. 5 (May 1911): 483.
313. White, "Richmond Locomotive Builders," 84.

5. The Boulevard Expansion and World War I, 1869–1917

314. *Daily Dispatch*, April 25, 1870.
315. *Richmond Dispatch*, May 4, 1893.
316. *Iron Age* 49 (June 1892): 1232.
317. *Richmond Dispatch*, June 2, 1892.
318. *Richmond Dispatch*, March 1, 1893.
319. *The Times*, December 15, 1892.
320. *Richmond Dispatch*, September 29, 1894; *Times Dispatch*, March 24, 1910.
321. *Richmond Dispatch*, February 7, 1892; Matthew R. Laird, *Archaeological Data Recovery Investigation of The Lumpkin's Jail Site (44HE1053) Richmond, Virginia* (Williamsburg, VA: James River Institute for Archaeology, 2010), 28.
322. *Richmond Dispatch*, February 6, 1892; Sanborn Map, 1895; *Richmond Dispatch*, September 22, 1907.
323. Sanborn Maps, 1895, 1905, LOC.
324. Laird, *Archaeological Data Recovery Investigation*, 28.
325. *Richmond Dispatch*, April 11, 1900.
326. *The Times*, May 6, 1900.
327. *The Times*, May 30, 1902; *Richmond Dispatch*, June 4, 1902.
328. Elmer T. Howson, D.A. Steel, and J.B. Tebo, *The Biographical Directory of the Railway Officials of America 1922 Edition* (New York: Simmons-Boardman, 1922), 140.
329. *Richmond Dispatch*, June 4, 1902.
330. *The Times*, October 15, 1902; *Times-Dispatch*, June 8, 1905.
331. *The Times*, May 31, 1900.
332. *Times-Dispatch*, December 15, 1907; Sanborn Map, 1908.
333. *Times-Dispatch*, September 22, 1907.

334. *Times-Dispatch*, June 13, 1908.
335. Howson, Steel, and Tebo, *Biographical Directory*, 140.
336. *Richmond Virginian*, March 31, 1910.
337. *Times Dispatch*, October 30, 1910; *Times Dispatch*, June 28, 1910; *Eighth Annual Report of the State Corporation Commission of Virginia, for the Year Ending December 31, 1910* (Richmond, VA: Davis Bottom, 1911), 104.
338. *Times-Dispatch*, July 3, 1910.
339. *Times-Dispatch*, October 30, 1910.
340. Ibid.
341. *Times-Dispatch*, April 2, 1911.
342. *Times Dispatch*, April 14, 1913.
343. Ibid.; *Times-Dispatch*, April 2, 1911
344. *Richmond Virginian*, November 5, 1910.
345. *Times-Dispatch*, March 22, 1911.
346. *Times-Dispatch*, April 2, 1911.
347. *Richmond Virginian*, May 25, 1911; *Times-Dispatch*, May 28, 1911.
348. *Mathews (VA) Journal*, June 1, 1911.
349. *Times-Dispatch*, July 16, 1911.
350. Richmond Iron Works to Charles Evans Wingo (January 25, 1912), Wingo Family Papers, Mss1 W7277 b 418-453, VMHC.
351. *Times-Dispatch*, February 22, 1912; *Times-Dispatch*, February 14, 1912; *Times-Dispatch*, May 4, 1913.
352. *Times-Dispatch*, November 9, 1913; *Richmond Virginian*, January 23, 1914.
353. RLW Account Book, inventory 1899, VMHC.
354. *Evening Journal*, March 30, 1915; *Times-Dispatch*, April 7, 1915; *News Leader*, April 8, 1915.
355. Martin Horn, "A Private Bank at War: J.P. Morgan & Co. and France, 1914–1918," *Business History Review* 74, no. 1 (2000): 85.
356. *Richmond Virginian*, April 17, 1915; *Times-Dispatch*, April 18, 1915.
357. "Participation of the Richmond Works of the American Locomotive Company in the Late World War," Virginia War History Commission City Source Material, 1919–1927, 37219, Box 75, Folder 19, LVA, 1.
358. Ibid., 2.
359. Ibid., 4–5.
360. *Times-Dispatch*, February 5, 1917.
361. "Participation of the Richmond Works," 5.
362. *The Financier* 55, no. 1672 (August 5, 1916): 362; *The Financier* 55, no. 1673 (August 12, 1916): 430.
363. *Times-Dispatch*, April 22, 1917.

364. Bryan Clark Green, "Richmond Locomotive and Machine Works," National Register of Historic Places Nomination Form (Washington, D.C.: U.S. Department of the Interior, National Park Service, 2006), Section 8.

6. A Return to Locomotives and the End of the Line, 1917–1927

365. "Participation of the Richmond Works," 10.
366. Ibid, 11.
367. *Times-Dispatch*, July 1, 1917.
368. ALCO Annual Report, 1917, 8.
369. *New York Sun*, August 26, 1917; *Times-Dispatch*, November 20, 1918; *Journal of the American Society of Mechanical Engineers* 40, no. 8 (August 1918): 702; ALCO Annual Report 1931.
370. *Evening Journal*, August 26, 1918.
371. *Richmond Planet*, April 27, 1918.
372. *Richmond Planet*, June 19, 1897.
373. *Evening Journal*, October 27, 1918.
374. "Participation of the Richmond Works," 12.
375. Joseph Bryan to S.R. Callaway (October 15, 1903), VMHC.
376. ALCO Annual Report 1919, 10.
377. Ibid.
378. *Manufacturers Record* 82, no. 16 (October 1922): 55.
379. Douglas B. Craig, "'Don't You Hear all the Railroad Men Squeak?': William G. McAdoo, the United States Railroad Administration, and the Democratic Presidential Nomination of 1924," *Journal of American Studies* 48, no. 3 (August 2014): 779–80.
380. Brian Solomon, *ALCO Locomotives* (Minneapolis, MN: MBI Publishing Company, 2009), 43.
381. "Participation of the Richmond Works," 11.
382. *News Leader*, July 9, 1918.
383. *Times-Dispatch*, July 8, 1922.
384. ALCO Annual Report 1928, 10.
385. O.M. Kerr, *Illustrated Treasury of the American Locomotive Company* (Alburg, VT: Delta, 1980), 9; *Power Wagon* 104 (July 1, 1913): 72; *Times-Dispatch*, August 23, 1913.
386. Albert J. Churella, *From Steam to Diesel: Managerial Customs and Organizational Capabilities in the Twentieth-Century American Locomotive Industry* (Princeton, NJ: Princeton University Press, 1998), 14.

387. Kerr, *Illustrated Treasury*, 10.
388. Churella, *From Steam to Diesel*, 19.
389. Ibid., 20.
390. *Railroad Age Gazette* 47, no. 11 (September 1909): 447.
391. *Evening Journal*, August 11, 1913.
392. *Times-Dispatch*, February 19, 1917.
393. *Evening Journal*, May 10, 1917.
394. *Railway and Locomotive Engineering* 30, no. 3 (March 1917): 103; *News Leader*, January 18, 1917.
395. *Catalogue 1921–1922 of the Virginia Mechanics Institute*, 14; *Evening Journal*, July 13, 1914; *News Leader*, July 22, 1913.
396. *New York Herald*, April 23, 1922; *American Machinist* 58, no. 10 (March 1923): 391.
397. *Times-Dispatch*, August 20, 1919; *Times-Dispatch*, October 22, 1920.
398. White, "Richmond Locomotive Builders," 85.
399. *News Leader*, August 2, 1923.
400. White, "Richmond Locomotive Builders," 86.
401. *Times-Dispatch*, February 11, 1908; *Railway Age Gazette* 59 (New York: Simmons-Boardman Publishing Company, 1915), 477; *American Engineer: The Railway Mechanical Monthly* 86 (New York: Simmons-Boardman Publishing Company, 1912), 105.
402. *News Leader*, November 8, 1935.
403. Churella, *From Steam to Diesel*, 4.
404. Ibid., 10.
405. Kerr, *Illustrated Treasury*, 14, 22.
406. Ibid., 15–17.
407. Ibid., 18.
408. Fairbanks Morse Defense, https://www.fairbanksmorse.com/251f.

7. Legacies, 1927 to the Present

409. Madison, *Tredegar Iron Works*, 163.
410. Barber, *Tyrrell Timber*, 122–24.
411. ALCO Annual Report 1949, 6; *Times-Dispatch*, June 30, 1949.
412. *News Leader*, July 4, 1949.
413. *Times-Dispatch*, March 15, 1931.
414. *News Leader*, February 22, 1933.
415. *Railway Age* 94, no. 15 (April 1933): 568.

416. *Times-Dispatch*, July 26, 1942.
417. *News Leader*, April 8, 1936. The article in question states that the site was "purchased"; however, as both later articles and ALCO's own report to its stockholders in 1949 attest to the site being offered for sale, in addition to the Accessories Plant listed as ALCO property in annual reports after 1936, it seems most likely that the period between 1936 and 1950 saw the Brooks Company only leasing the facilities.
418. William B. Foster Jr., "Brooks Celebrates Its 75th Year," *Commonwealth* 20, no. 1 (January 1953): 17–18.
419. Jeff Brooks, in discussion with the author, July 2022.
420. *News Leader*, April 8, 1930.
421. *News Leader*, December 22, 1937.
422. *Times-Dispatch*, April 22, 1938.
423. *Times-Dispatch*, April 29, 1938.
424. *Times-Dispatch*, May 24, 1938.
425. *News Leader*, February 10, 1939.
426. Marie Tyler-McGraw, *At the Falls: Richmond, Virginia, and Its People* (Chapel Hill: University of North Carolina Press, 1994), 272; *News Leader*, February 10, 1949; *Times-Dispatch*, July 30, 1950.
427. *Times-Dispatch*, May 7, 1942.
428. The RECO Story: Past-Present-Future presentation, by Bob Courain, courtesy of Shamrock Environmental, 2022.
429. Claude Burrows, "191-Ton Locomotive, City Relic, Awaits Smithsonian Resting Place," *Times Dispatch*, March 16, 1962.
430. Burke Davis, *The Southern Railway: Roads of the Innovators* (Chapel Hill: University of North Carolina Press, 1985), 214.
431. Warden, "Richmond Locomotive Works," 25.

INDEX

P

R

S

T

U

V

W

ABOUT THE AUTHOR

Nathan Vernon Madison is a graduate of the University of Mary Washington (BA) and Virginia Commonwealth University (MA). His works on Richmond industry include *Tredegar Iron Works: Richmond's Foundry on the James* (2015) and a chronicle of industrial Richmond for the Society for Industrial Archaeology (2018). He has participated in or coproduced documentaries airing on PBS, C-SPAN, AMC, and the BBC. He also writes and lectures on the history of popular literature, his books and articles regarding this topic published by Routledge, ABC/CLIO, and McFarland; he also serves on the editorial board of the Pulp Magazines Project, an academic digital repository dedicated to preserving late nineteenth- and early twentieth-century popular literature. He is a member of the Society for Industrial Archaeology and the Society for Historians of the Gilded Age and Progressive Era.